THE LITTLE BOOK OF
ENGLISH RUGBY

Written by Jed Smith

THE LITTLE BOOK OF
ENGLISH RUGBY

This edition first published in the UK in 2006
By Green Umbrella

© Green Umbrella Publishing 2006

www.greenumbrella.co.uk

Publishers Jules Gammond & Vanessa Gardner

Printed and bound in China

ISBN-13: 978-1-905828-08-1
ISBN-10: 1-905828-08-X

Contents

From a green field in Warwickshire

"you don't know the rules – you'll be a month learning them… there's been two collar bones broken this half, and a dozen fellows lamed"
Thomas Hughes, 'Tom Brown's School Days', 1857

ABOVE Martin Johnson gets his hands on rugby's ultimate prize

THE MORNING OF Saturday 22 November 2003 was miserable. The sky was battleship grey, the wind was chill and the drizzle was endless. But what a wonderful day to be alive! On the other side of the planet, in the backyard of those arch-sledgers Australia, the England rugby team had lifted the Rugby World Cup trophy – the first side from the northern hemisphere to break the Australia/South Africa/New Zealand stranglehold on the event. Dewey-eyed poems were destined to be written that day. Work would start on embroidery, painting and collage. Car horns would be hooted at an empty Twickenham Stadium as proud English rugby followers looked for ways to celebrate and commemorate; to be part of the great event.

It was wonderfully appropriate that the captain, Martin Johnson, was the first English player to lift the trophy. Johnson was the latest in a long line of English captains who led from the

front by example; a lineage of powerful, Grand Slam-winning forwards who led by deed rather than word, that can be traced back through Beaumont, Evans, Cove-Smith, Wakefield and Wodehouse. He was also English Midlands through and through, having been born in Solihull, only 20 miles from the site of the game's development: Rugby School, a public school in the Warwickshire market town of the same name.

The development of rugby football, as with so many other things that we presume to understand clearly, is shrouded in mystery, conjecture and no little myth. As with all other football codes, rugby football derived from medieval games where a ball could be kicked, carried and thrown; and in which the players were able to do pretty much anything that they damn well pleased, including full contact, full-bloodied, tackling. A description of these games in 1518 as being "a devilish pastime… sometimes brawling, murder, homicide and great effusion of blood" provides us with a wonderfully

vivid indication of the violent and unruly mayhem that ensued before English public schoolboys started to create order out of the chaos in the early nineteenth century.

Even older traces of rugby's ancestry can be discerned, such as the Roman game of Harpestum (meaning 'to snatch') where two teams of players fought for possession of a ball in a marked out area and attempted to carry it over the opposition's goal line. What the Rugby schoolboys did was to create a version of medieval football that suited their environment, playing numbers and traditions. The same thing was happening, quite independently, in the other English public schools.

The first commonly-held misconception to be laid to rest is the idea that this word 'football' refers to modern football or 'soccer'. The confusion often arises due to the misleading phraseology of the late nineteenth century William Webb Ellis myth and the subsequent belief that he created a brand new game whilst playing soccer. At the time the term 'football' was applied to any team game where a ball was kicked or thrown around the field. The Rugby School game still proudly carries the moniker of rugby football, is governed in England by the Rugby Football Union and played by rugby footballers. It was only when soccer (association football) became Britain's pre-eminent winter sport that it grabbed the word 'football' for its own, seemingly exclusive, use.

Back at Rugby School the boys themselves were managing and governing their own version of football. They refereed it themselves, with no assistance from the school masters, and argued over potential law changes. These changes were debated by the senior boys on 'the island' a small prehistoric mound in the School grounds which can still be seen today and should, by rights, be the ultimate place of pilgrimage for any lover of the game. Rule changes came and went and then came again. It was a fluid situation that allowed for innovation, alteration and untold changes of mind.

New boys learned the rules by watching – and whilst doing so they were co-opted into acting as goal keepers, in an attempt to keep the opposition's players away from the goal line they defended.

The rules were never written down anywhere and, quite honestly, there was no need to. The game was only played at Rugby School itself or by fully-informed former Rugby Schoolboys. However, it

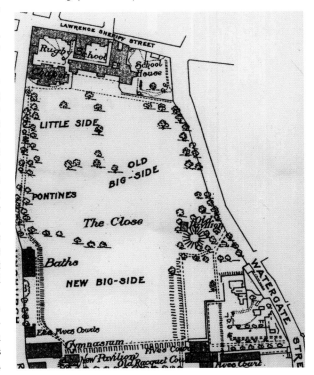

BELOW Plan of Rugby School. The Island, where rule changes were made, is next to the Old Pavilion to the right of The Close

was the growth of the game beyond Rugby School that initially allowed it to survive and then ultimately to flourish. This growth can be attributed to three factors and to a couple of Arnolds.

Dr Thomas Arnold was headmaster at Rugby School throughout the entire 1830s and was responsible for the creation of a revolutionary educational model that put religion at the very centre of school life. Arnold's philosophy of education is sometimes referred to as 'muscular Christianity' and it placed equal emphasis on a healthy body and a healthy mind.

The theory worked wonderfully in practice and the rest of the country followed suit. New Public Schools were being set up in the middle of the nineteenth century to facilitate the education of England's burgeoning middle classes, and many of them (Marlborough, Cheltenham, Wellington, Haileybury, etc…) were created just as Arnold's theories were at their zenith. With the diffusion of the educational model came the diffusion of Arnold's staff and former

BELOW Fighting for possession of the ball at Rugby School in the 1840s

pupils around the country and with them went the Rugby School football game that perfectly embodied his ideal of tough, honest, self sacrificing 'muscular Christian' boys.

Word of mouth would only affect limited results, however, and the first ever written rules of any football code, drawn up at Rugby School in 1845, were the catalyst for ensuring that the Rugby School football game was easy to spread. This time a different Arnold was involved. One of the three boys who drew up the laws was William, one of the Doctor's sons. These laws did not provide a comprehensive A-Z of the game, but instead gave reference points for the 37 rules considered most contentious and in need of clarification.

The final piece in the jigsaw arrived in 1857 with the publication of Thomas Hughes' semi-autobiographical 'Tom Brown's School Days'. Hughes had been a former captain of football at Rugby School and in the much loved book he depicted the game of the 1830s when

BELOW The earliest photograph of rugby football, showing two large teams

many familiar features (H-shaped goals, enormous rolling mauls, an off-side rule and a touch down allowing a player to 'try a kick at goal') had already evolved. The novel was a hugely popular bestseller – one of the definitive works of the period – and the description of the young Tom Brown being knocked out cold whilst defending his side's goal line placed the Rugby School game firmly into the public's consciousness.

These three factors placed the game in good stead and allow it to stand alone when the other English public school football games were amalgamated to create the dribbling-only 'soccer' game in 1863.

Despite the verdict given by John Thring in the 1840s that "It would be quite impossible to induce different schools to give up their time honoured vanities and adopt a uniform game" this desire became increasingly apparent as boys strove to create compromise rules when playing with each other at university. The Cambridge Rules of 1848 were such a compromise between the different public school football rules. Alternatively, teams would play one half of a game by each other's rules or alternate between their differing rules.

RIGHT Dr Thomas Arnold

BELOW An illustration from 'Tom Brown's School Days' by Thomas Hughes

A mild annoyance at university became a major gripe once these football-playing boys entered the working world and set up the first football clubs around the country. Richmond flirted with Rugby football, Harrow football and Association football (depending upon which players were available for selection and who they were playing on any given day) before finally settling on rugby.

The aforementioned Association football was the result of a concerted attempt in 1863 to set up a national set of football rules that everyone could

play outside of the public schools – since there was little hope that the schools themselves would be persuaded to give up their own loyally held games. A series of meetings led to the formation of the Football Association (FA). Representatives of the various public schools (including Rugby School) were, sure enough, not at the FA's meetings; being quite happy to continue playing their own football games.

After much discussion the FA based their new laws on the Cambridge Rules of 1848 which had outlawed 'hacking'. Kicking an opponent's shins with sharpened boots might strike us as particularly barbaric, even if that same opponent was stubbornly holding onto the ball, but the act was an integral part of the Rugby School game where it was seen as yet another way of testing 'manliness' on the field.

By our standards the Rugby School game of the time was nothing less than legalised thuggery. The previous season the Blackheath club had found it necessary to remind their members that throttling or strangling an opponent was "totally opposed to the principles of the game" although hacking below the

ABOVE Francis Campbell of Blackheath

knee was fine. The members of the fledgling FA struggled to see how painful hacking injuries would in any way assist them in their professional careers now that they had left school.

Although they had agreed to allow handling the ball in their early rules, the FA voted against hacking and the Blackheath Club representative, Francis Campbell, walked out. In effect he took all Rugby School footballers with him. "If you do away with it [hacking] you will do away with all the courage and pluck of the game, and I will be bound to bring over a lot of Frenchmen who will beat you with a week's practice" suggested Campbell, pointedly, as he made his excuses.

Ignoring what Campbell's line tells us about the way that Victorian men associated the French with effeminacy, his act was possibly the most important in the game's long and rich history. It is tempting to wonder what might have happened had he not walked. Rugby School football would probably have gone the same way as Winchester and Charterhouse football – ultimately usurped by the all-powerful soccer game that they had helped to create. Soccer itself may well have been

a joint handling/dribbling code uniting all clubs under one banner and preventing the necessity for a separately governed sport.

As it was, the new game of soccer retained only a few traces of the original handling/dribbling compromise (goal keepers, throw-ins, etc...) and did not really take off during the 1860s. It was during the following decade that soccer and rugby finally exploded in popularity and the various other public school football games were condemned to obscurity.

For a while there was still hope that a compromise could be reached that would allow the two sides to come together to create a genuinely all-encompassing set of football rules. Being outcasts and not having their game governed or controlled was of no great concern to the supporters of the Rugby School game and clubs continued to spring up throughout England in the 1860s. The problem was that more clubs meant more variations on the rules. Minds finally turned towards the creation of a similar body to the FA in late 1870 after criticism in the press about the violent nature of rugby football. The situation was exacerbated

following the death of a player in a trial match at Richmond.

A second administrative body for football was created in early 1871. This time it was a body (or Union) for the Rugby School football game – the Rugby Football Union (RFU). With this creation the split between rugby football and association football was cemented. The Association clubs would eventually inherit the word 'football' in England leaving most member clubs of the RFU to insert the word 'rugby' into their names to avoid confusion.

An English sporting revolution had occurred, but no-one yet realised how important it would be.

ABOVE Forwards pushing and shoving in a large scrum, 1871

A body to regulate the game

RIGHT First minutes of the Rugby Football Union

BELOW Leonard Maton

"An opinion has for some time prevailed among the supporters of Rugby football that some code should be adopted by all clubs who profess to play the Rugby game."
Edwin Ash [Richmond] and Benjamin Burns [Blackheath], 1870

ON 24 DECEMBER 1870 A LETTER from the Richmond and Blackheath clubs appeared in the press which ultimately led to the creation of the RFU - a governing body for the rugby game.

The first meeting was held at the old Pall Mall restaurant in London, the current site of the Texas Embassy restaurant, which carries a blue plaque to commemorate the event. The first raft of member clubs came exclusively from suburban London and the first minute taken at that January 1871 meeting declared that "the society be called the 'Rugby Football Union'". The Union's first set of laws outlawed hacking, although that did not prevent renegade teams of former public schoolboys from getting together for games where hacking was allowed. That they would hobble from the field was of no concern. In some quarters a hacking scar was still a proudly worn badge of courage - the equivalent of a duelling scar.

One of the RFU Committee, Wimbledon Hornets' Leonard Maton,

It was then proposed by Mr. A. G. Guillemard (West Kent) and seconded by Mr. W. F. Eaton (Ravenscourt), and carried unanimously That the Society be called the "Rugby Football Union".

was incapacitated at the time with a broken leg and so he drafted the first RFU laws whilst his companions kept him supplied with tobacco.

Although formed in England, the initial intention was that the RFU would be a governing body for the whole game, worldwide. Membership was not to be restricted to English clubs and schools, hence the lack of a letter 'E' anywhere in the initials. In 1873, when the first breakaway Union was formed in Scotland, the RFU's membership already included five clubs in Scotland and Ireland. From that point onwards, as other unions were formed, the RFU started to become an English national union by default, although it was still to be joined in subsequent years by member clubs from New Zealand, South Africa, Hong Kong, India, Wales, USA, Canada and Australia. Within four years of its foundation the RFU already had over 100 clubs in membership.

Having approved Maton's set of laws to eradicate the different interpretations

21 FOUNDER MEMBER CLUBS OF THE RUGBY FOOTBALL UNION

Addison	(no longer in existence)
Belsize Park	(no longer in existence)
Blackheath	
Civil Service	
Clapham Rovers	(no longer in existence)
Flamingoes	(no longer in existence)
Guy's Hospital	(now Guy's, King's and St. Thomas' Hospital)
Gipsies	(no longer in existence)
Harlequins	
King's College	(now Guy's, King's and St. Thomas' Hospital)
Lausanne	(no longer in existence)
Law Club	(no longer in existence)
Marlborough Nomads	(no longer in existence)
Mohicans	(no longer in existence)
Queen's House	(no longer in existence)
Ravenscourt Park	(no longer in existence)
Richmond	
St Paul's School	
Wellington College	
West Kent	(no longer in existence)
Wimbledon Hornets	(now Wimbledon)

FOOTBALL MATCH BETWEEN ENGLAND AND SCOTLAND.

On Monday the great football match, "England versus Scotland," was played at Edinburgh in the presence of a large number of spectators. The twenties pitted against each other were the representatives of the best clubs in the two countries. The game was keenly contested, and during the first fifty minutes both sides touched down and were equal. After changing sides, the Scotch twenty invaded the quarters of the English and became entitled to a try. The kick off resulted in a goal being obtained. The English twenty afterwards got a try, but failed to obtain a goal. After a hard struggle the Scotch team again got a touch down in the English ground, but did not succeed in obtaining a goal with their try. Time being then up, the Scotch were declared the winners by a goal and a touch down

ABOVE Report of the very first international rugby match - Scotland v England, 1871

at large in the game, the next concern was to arrange the first ever international rugby match in response to a challenge from Scottish clubs. It was to be within the international game that rugby was to find its greatest strength.

The first ever international rugby fixture lacked the enormous fanfare that a match of that status generates today. Scotland versus England on 27 March 1871 earned only 16 lines of coverage, towards the back of 'The Penny Illustrated Paper', sandwiched tightly between discussions about athletic club meetings in the London area.

The twenty English players; this being six years before numbers were reduced to 15 a-side; are reputed to have travelled up to Edinburgh overnight, sitting on wooden boards in third class carriages. Some of the better English players were not able to attend, due to the short notice, whilst the Scots had been able to engage in a practice session. If that wasn't enough, the Scots had home advantage in front of 4,000 spectators and used a narrow pitch to their tactical advantage. A try that was disputed by the English contingent – there were still a variety of interpretations in the game – ultimately defeated England.

The referee (also Scottish) waved away English complaints about the Scottish try, declaring that "when an umpire is in doubt, I think he is justified in deciding against the side that makes the most noise. They are probably in the wrong". In the days before point scoring

was introduced the result was 'one goal and one try to one goal' - in other words a converted try and an unconverted try against a converted try. It wasn't an encouraging start for the team in white.

The white jersey and red rose emblem with matching white shorts was in place from the very beginning. The white was taken from the white kit worn at Rugby School and it is said that for a time the England captain was obliged to ask the Rugby School football captain for permission to use the white jersey. The derivation of the red rose is less easy to pinpoint. Red roses feature on the Rugby School coat of arms, but it may equally have been selected as a reference to the fact that the rose (albeit a red and white rose) is England's national flower.

England team v
Ireland, 1878. England's
fourth match as a team
of 15 a-side and the first
international fixture held
at Lansdowne Road

Fixtures between England and
Scotland were played annually, alter-
nating between the two countries.
This decision set a template which is
still in place today in the modern Six
Nations tournament despite all that
has changed since. Rugby is nothing if
not a lover of tradition. The most significant change of the period was the
aforementioned reduction from 20 to
15 players-a-side. Pioneered by Oxford
and Cambridge Universities in 1875,
the attacking advantages of reduced

playing numbers were obvious and
other clubs quickly adopted the new
formation. Initially, teams would field
two full backs, two three-quarters, two
half-backs and a pack of nine forwards. Although one of the full-backs
soon became a three-quarter it was not
until 1894 that England copied the
Welsh example by moving a forward
backwards to play with four three-
quarters. The system has remained
unchanged since.

The introduction of the Calcutta Cup

instead to provide the RFU with a trophy that could be used as an equivalent to soccer's FA Cup: "…a Challenge Cup… to be competed for annually in the same way as the Association Cup…". That particular competition was proving immensely popular with spectators but the RFU committee was aware that a national club knockout competition would raise the spectre of over-competitiveness with clubs possibly tempted to do anything in their power to win, rather than playing the game for the game's sake. The newly acquired silver-ware would be used for inter-national competition instead. By 1879 only one further coun-try had raised an international team – Ireland. However, they had yet to score a single point in any of their matches or to face Scotland and so by default the Calcutta Cup became the England v Scotland trophy.

The lack of impact of the early Irish sides was not helped by the coexistence of two distinct Irish Unions operating in the North and South. The very first Irish out-ing, against England at

for England v Scotland matches in 1879 spiced up the annual fixture and pro-vided a competitive focus that still res-onates today. When the Calcutta Club in India had been forced to abandon the game due to falling playing numbers they presented a trophy to the RFU as a lasting memorial to their club. They would scarcely have believed how suc-cessful their endeavour has been.

Less well known is that they did not intend for the trophy to be used at the annual England v Scotland clash, but

LEFT The Calcutta Cup
BELOW A N 'Monkey' Hornby

Kennington Oval in 1875, had been an easy English victory. Of the twenty Irish players, ten had been chosen by each of the two unions, a selection policy not destined to catch on. A single Irish Rugby Football Union would be formed in 1879.

When Wales fielded their first side in 1881 their try line was breached 13 times by England to no reply. The shock of such a hammering forced the Welsh to act quickly and the Welsh Rugby Union was formed some three weeks later.

A character who perfectly symbolised the era was Albert 'Monkey' Hornby. He happened to be a very capable cricketer who captained the England Test team against Australia when the idea of The Ashes was created. He was also England rugby captain in 1882 but had to respectfully decline an invitation to play for England against Scotland the following season because it was 'most inconvenient' as it would interfere with his shooting 'which was going particularly well' at the time!

Typical attendances for international matches during the period were very low by later standards. Only 3,000 turned up in Manchester in 1883 to see England defeat Ireland whilst a paltry 2,000 witnessed the victory over Wales in Leeds the following season. Regular international attendances in excess of 10,000 would not be seen until the 1890s.

A key season in many respects was 1884. It was the first time that all four home unions played against each other in a single season – a first appearance of the embryonic Four/Five/Six Nations Championship. The 'Championship' was never actually envisaged as such by anyone involved. It was the press who first started to create tables, name champions and determine wooden spoon 'winners' from the annual series of friendly matches that the countries played.

BELOW One of the very first examples of a 'Championship' table, from 1893

		W.	L.	D.		G.	T.	P.		G.	T.	P.
1.	Wales....................	3	0	0	scored	3	6	23	lost	1	3	11
2.	Scotland	1	1	1	,,	2	0	8	,,	1	3	9
3.	England	1	2	0	,,	1	5	15	,,	4	2	20
4.	Ireland	0	2	1	,,	0	0	0	,,	0	3	6

On the field England had started to employ the tactical passing game that had been developed at Oxford University by Harry Vassall, whose University side lost only twice in seventy matches during the early 1880s. Previously, the fashion had been for a player to run as far as they could with the ball before being caught and tackled.

In previous decades the idea of passing had been likened to an act of cowardice – as if a player was not prepared to accept the pain of the impending tackle! The net effect of passing was to open up the game and do away with the ten minute mauls that had typified the game up until then. The introduction of the law that compelled a tackled player to release the ball in 1887 served to further increase this development.

Another massively important event took place in 1884 although no-one could have foreseen the implications at the time. England's winning try against

ABOVE Harry Vassall sitting in the front middle of the 1882 Oxford University side. He had scored three tries on his England debut the previous year, in a 13 try demolition of Wales

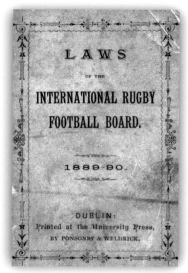

LAWS
OF THE
INTERNATIONAL RUGBY
FOOTBALL BOARD.

1889-90.

DUBLIN:
Printed at the University Press,
BY PONSONBY & WELDRICK.

ABOVE An early IRFB handbook from before the RFU accepted their authority

Scotland that season was disputed and led to an off field face-off that Scotland suggested should be settled by an independent adjudicator. The reply, from RFU Secretary, George Rowland Hill, was cutting: "my (RFU) Committee… regret that they are unable to acknowledge any higher court of appeal in connection with the construction of the laws of the game, which they themselves framed"

In other words, this is our game, we drew up the rules and if you don't like them you can go off and play something else. Unsurprisingly this response only served to aggravate the situation and in 1886 Scotland, Ireland and Wales went ahead and created the independent body that they thought was needed - the International Rugby Football Board (IRFB). The RFU refused to accept or join the new body and were therefore denied any fixtures

against the other three nations for two seasons. In 1890 a compromise was reached: the other three unions would each have two seats on the IRFB whilst England were granted the six seats required to give them the power of veto over anything not to their taste. This imbalance remained in place for a further twenty years.

At first the IRFB (which dropped the 'Football' to become the IRB in 1998) were solely responsible for the laws pertaining to international matches whilst the individual unions administered their own clubs. The international fixture programme was back on again and the first IRFB act was to introduce a standard point scoring system for international matches (one point for a try, two for a conversion and three for a dropped goal or penalty).

This removed the inconsistencies in the game. England's two tries in Scotland in March 1890 scored by Frank Evershed (a solicitor playing at Blackheath) and Jack Dyson (a publican playing at Huddersfield) had gained two points each under Scottish Rugby Union laws, However, a couple of weeks later England's three tries at home to Ireland were only worth one point each under RFU laws.

Another challenge to the RFU's authority came from a less likely source – its own clubs. Until the 1870s rugby was a game that only the upper and middle classes had the time or opportunity to play in their exclusive suburban clubs dotted around the country. However, the growing popularity of team sports had led to the adoption of the game amongst the English working classes. Working men now had, for the first time and thanks to government legislation in the 1870s, free time available to them on Saturdays (God help anyone who had ever considered playing sport on a Sunday!). As pubs, churches and factories started to organise their own teams rugby football started to drift away from the clutches of the former public school boys and the gentleman amateurs.

The working man particularly took to rugby since it utilised strength and provided physical confrontation. Now it was in the industrial conurbations of northern England, where the success of the local team was tied up in civic pride, that the English game's powerbase lay. Northern rugby was passionately territorial and winning meant everything.

ABOVE Lancashire 'Baines' card

The prestigious Yorkshire Cup competition, which was played for from 1877 onwards, attracted crowds in the tens of thousands and the finals were a bigger draw than international rugby or even soccer's FA Cup final.

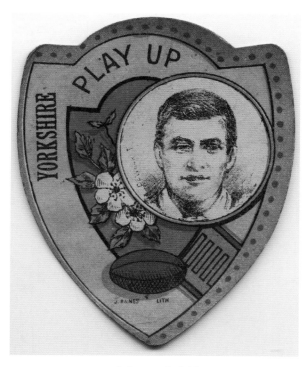

ABOVE Yorkshire 'Baines' card

band and an immense concourse of people, and marched from the station to the Woolpacks Inn, the cheering in the streets being again and again renewed."

The growth of professionalism in the game had never been an issue when the players were exclusively ex-public school-boys. The middle classes, with their public school ideals, expected the working class players to copy their amateur values, but playing sport for money was normal in working class life and they did not expect to play an increasingly popular spectator sport for nothing.

The first documented example of a rugby player being paid was Teddy Bartram in 1879 and the slow rise of 'veiled professionalism' in certain English clubs continued to build through the 1880s. It was stimulated by the regional cup competitions and if a club was anxious to stay at the top of the tree there was an obvious cycle to follow. Cup success led to larger crowds which meant more money being taken on the turnstile. These gate receipts provided funds to invest in 'attracting' good players from other clubs which would then lead to further cup success.

When Wakefield Trinity won the cup in 1879, the whole city celebrated:

"the Parish Church bells began to ring in honour of the event. On the arrival at Wakefield of the special train, the victors were met by the Church

Funds were initially provided to reimburse existing players for lost wages (whilst training, playing, travelling to matches, injured, etc…) but it was soon extended to offering financial inducements to entice players from other clubs. The RFU were actually powerless to combat the spread until 1886 because they did not have any laws relating to professionalism; so sure were the early pioneers that it would never be an issue in their game. Once these laws were framed the punishments began in earnest, including the life banning of the aforementioned Bartram. All-out war was just around the corner. "No mercy but iron rigour will be dealt out", articulated RFU Committee man Arthur Budd in 1886.

"What the working man requires is hard cash for services rendered, and in view of the money the clubs make, his demand is fair and legitimate" (AA Sutherland, former Salford and Swinton player, 1894)

BELOW Yorkshire v Lancashire at Huddersfield in 1891

LONDON AND NORTH WESTERN RAILWAY.

FOOTBALL MATCH

AT LEEDS.

BATLEY v. HUNSLET.

CHEAP EXCURSION TICKETS

WILL BE ISSUED TO

LEEDS

On SATURDAY, March 13, 1897,

AS UNDER:—

STATIONS.	Times of Starting.	FARE—Third Class.
BATLEY ....depart	p.m. 1 30	10D.
LEEDS ....arrive	1 52	

Returning from LEEDS at 6.20 p.m. the same day.

If the Football Match is postponed this Excursion will not run.

Children under 3 years of age free; above 3 and under 12 half-fares. No Luggage allowed. Tickets not Transferable.

FRED. HARRISON, General Manager.

ABOVE Advertising handbill for a 1897 Northern Union game

The northern English clubs were not necessarily pushing for full professionalism but they wanted to pay money for loss of earnings ('broken time'). This compromise found no favour with the RFU. How, they countered, would a London team attracting far fewer supporters afford to pay the lost wages of 15 solicitors, businessmen and doctors?

Besides this the RFU were desperate to maintain amateurism as a matter of principle because they felt that the game was theirs. If professionalism had been allowed to run rife the well-to-do players (i.e. themselves) could not have hoped to compete against teams of fully prepared professionals. They and their clubs would have lost control of their game, and they were not prepared to let that happen. They had a perfect case study at hand in soccer where amateur clubs like Old Etonians had dominated the early years of the FA Cup but were now outplayed by professional big city clubs and fading into obscurity.

Citing a desire to see the game played exclusively for the love of it (despite evidence that these same amateurs were not above cheating, arguing or blatant gamesmanship) and not for material gain they took on the dissenting clubs, who were mostly based in Lancashire and Yorkshire, and left them nowhere to turn.

"If blind enthusiasts of working men's clubs insist on introducing professionalism, there can be but one result - disunion"
(Arthur Budd, RFU Committee, 1892)

In August 1895 21 RFU clubs met in Huddersfield and formed a breakaway body - the Northern Rugby Football Union, commonly referred to as the Northern Union. Within time the rival body would be called Rugby League and would go fully professional whilst also changing rugby's rules to make the game faster and simpler. In its initial seasons, however, the Northern Union clubs played RFU rules and only permitted the paying of 'broken time' money for a player's loss of earnings.

This initial trickle of clubs to the Northern Union became a flood. Within three years the 20 had become almost 100 and the RFU found itself in crisis. It can hardly be a coincidence that during these uncertain days, when the battle for 'ownership' of the game was so heated and the future looked so uncertain, that the old boys of Rugby School took it upon themselves to investigate the origins of their game. Despite the overwhelming evidence that the Rugby School game grew organically over several decades they came across a second hand story (lacking a shred of primary evidence to support it) of a boy named William Webb Ellis creating the running element of the game at Rugby School.

Other old boys who had been at the School at the time contradicted the story, but the investigators had found what all Victorians loved – a hero! The gradual evolution was forgotten when a plaque was erected at the School in 1900 and a 'big bang' story was created. The fact that the game was named after the School wasn't enough for them. By attaching the plaque naming Ellis and displaying 'a fine disregard for the rules

of evidence', they were sending out a very simple message – this is OUR game. But would there be any game left to govern if clubs continued to drift over to the Northern Union?

22 FOUNDER MEMBER CLUBS OF THE NORTHERN RUGBY FOOTBALL UNION

Batley	
Bradford	
Brighouse Rangers	(disbanded 1906)
Broughton Rangers	(disbanded 1955)
Halifax	
Huddersfield	
Hull	
Hunslet	
Leeds	
Leigh	
Liversedge	(disbanded 1901)
Manningham	(changed to Bradford City FC in 1903)
Oldham	
Rochdale Hornets	
Runcorn	(disbanded 1915)
St Helens	
Stockport	(disbanded 1903)
Tyldesley	(disbanded 1901)
Wakefield Trinity	
Warrington	
Widnes	
Wigan	

1896-1919

The fall and rise of the rose

"Rugby football in the North – for every part of the Kingdom in fact where there was a preponderance of working-class players – could not be honestly carried out under the existing bye-laws of the English Union"
Harry Waller, President of the Northern Union, 1896

IMMEDIATELY BEFORE THE schism of 1895 the RFU had a healthy 481 clubs in membership. By 1902 over half of that number had disappeared. The balance appeared to be moving in the Northern Union's favour and where would the drain end. How could the RFU prevent further English clubs, maybe even the vast majority, moving over to the Northern Union?

Lacking the desire to find a workable compromise the RFU decided to fight fire with fire. Their amateurism laws were strictly adhered to and anyone found playing for a Northern Union club would be banned from union for life. Even stepping onto a field with a known professional or training with one was enough to receive a lifetime's banishment.

So began a not-so-subtle whitewashing of history. If a player 'went North' they became persona-non-grata – no matter how spectacular their achieve-

ments in the union game. Fantastic players such as former England captain Dickie Lockwood (universally known as 'the world's little wonder' and a genuine candidate for canonisation in union history), Tom Broadley and Jack Toothill were all but airbrushed from RFU history. So was any subsequent mention of (statistically speaking) the greatest ever England team - the 1892 side who went an entire season without conceding a single point. That particu-

THE FALL AND RISE OF THE ROSE

lar England team featured 25 players, of whom 18 played for future Northern Union clubs and who therefore slipped out of union history.

For the next century English working men would, depending upon their regional location, tend to gravitate towards rugby league (as the Northern Union became known after 1922) or soccer. Certain areas stayed loyal to the RFU, most notably in the South West of England where the working men of Gloucester, Cornwall et al were dedicated to the game that provided regular contact with the great club sides of South Wales, whose close proximity to the region proved vitally important.

Despite such exceptions, rugby union (as rugby would eventually be called to differentiate it from league) in England was now to be increasingly perceived as an elitist game played exclusively by the well-to-do.

The drop in playing numbers led to an even greater drop in playing standards since the greatest English players of the pre-split period had hailed from the north where the embryonic County Championship competition had been dominated exclusively by Yorkshire and Lancashire. A disastrous series of results followed as the England team struggled to replace the absentees. Between 1896 and 1907 England won just 10 of the 40 matches they played and in four of the six seasons leading up to 1906 they lost all their fixtures.

With all of the four Home Unions now playing regular friendly fixtures against each other, journalists started to draw up tables to determine the leading nation. In the mid 1890s the first references to an international 'Championship' and 'wooden spoon' appeared, whilst the first reference to

THE FALL AND RISE OF THE ROSE

two or more teams.

England's problems were not confined to the playing field either. In 1909 CA Crane, the RFU President resigned from his position – the only such incumbent to so do. His RFU Committee had found Leicester innocent of fielding professional players and because he disagreed with the findings he resigned as a matter of honour. There was an enormous amount of interest in Leicester at the time. They were the top club side in the Midlands and the team who, if they had moved over to the Northern Union could quite conceivably have dragged most of the other midlands clubs with them – tipping the balance in the Northern Union's favour. This fact would have been as apparent to the RFU as it was to the Northern Union and might help to explain a certain leniency that Crane detected and resented.

The slump in England's fortunes happened to coincide with the visit of the first official touring sides from overseas. The rugby game had taken

LEFT Billy Wallace running in one of ten New Zealand tries v Gloucester in 1905

the 'triple crown' in a rugby context (the act of defeating the three other Home Unions in a single season to 'take' the three crowns from their heads) appeared in print in 1899. The modern tournament known to us as the Six Nations was slowly and organically growing, although the unions themselves would show little interest in it and refuse to acknowledge it with official status and a winner's trophy for another century. Since there was no official way to decide the winners of a tied 'Championship' many a season was shared between

ABOVE Springboks' Waltz song sheet

root all over the British Empire, and especially in the distant dominions of New Zealand, South Africa and Australia. Charles Munro introduced rugby into New Zealand after playing it at Christ's College, Finchley; whilst former England international player William Milton replaced Winchester School football with Rugby School football in the South African Cape. Rugby was an 'Empire' game and administrators, army officers, clergy and merchants took it around the world - hoping that it would teach and instil the qualities that they so admired. These counties were, for the moment at least, still very loyal to the union game and were also very adept at it. The first New Zealand 'All Blacks' administered a painful five try drubbing to England in 1905 and the first South African

'Springboks' did not lose any of the 17 matches they played on English soil the following year.

"They raced down the field, passing and repassing with bewildering speed and accuracy, and ultimately walked over the line unopposed, so completely had they outwitted the defence" (The Daily Mail reporting on the visiting South African team, 1906)

These countries had so very recently been the pupils, but were now the masters. All that English rugby could do was welcome the rejuvenating effect that every major visit had on the game at home.

Enormous crowds flocked to watch these masterful sides and when it was England's turn to face the first 'All Blacks' it was very obvious that the proposed venue at Blackheath was going to be insignificant to cope with the demand. The RFU hired the largest available venue, the Crystal Palace ground in south London, which is not to be confused with the soccer club of the same name. 45,000 was the official attendance, but in reality the figure was probably nearer to 80,000, not

Rugby Football Union.

Telegraphic Address:
"SCRUMMAGE, ..."
Twickenham

35, SURREY STREET,
STRAND, W.C.

January 8th 1910

DEAR SIR,

You have been selected to play for

England v. *Wales* at

Twickenham on *Saturday*

January 15th 1910.

Please let me know by ~~enclosed wire~~ return

if you can play.

Yours truly,

C. PERCIVAL COLES

Secretary.

VENUES FOR ENGLAND HOME MATCHES
1872-1910

Ground	Matches
Kennington Oval, London	7
Whalley Range, Manchester	7
Richardson's Field, Blackheath	1
Cardigan Fields, Leeds	1
Rectory Field, Blackheath	14
Crown Flatt, Dewsbury	1
Athletic Ground, Richmond	10
Headingley, Leeds	1
Birkenhead Park, Merseyside	1
Meanwood Road, Leeds	1
Fallowfield, Manchester	1
Kingsholm, Gloucester	1
Welford Road, Leicester	4
Crystal Palace, London	2
Ashton Gate, Bristol	1

including the many hundreds who climbed surrounding trees for a glimpse of the match. The game, as well as the equivalent fixture against the 1906 Springboks, was a great money spinner for the Union, but how much better would it have been if the RFU had a ground of their own, rather than having to hire? Since 1872 England had been playing home games all around the country, from London to Leeds, Manchester to

Bristol. Fifteen different venues had been used in all and it was argued by RFU Treasurer William Cail that the time was right to purchase.

A plot of land on the edge of Twickenham (it is actually located in neighbouring Whitton) in south west London was chosen and purchased in 1907. Although a risky venture in an unpromising location it would soon provide the perfect stage for the rejuvenation of the England team.

LEFT Ronnie Poulton-Palmer's invitation to play against Wales in 1910 - the first international match at Twickenham

ABOVE Twickenham in 1910

"Everyone will be wishing the Rugby Union and the game all prosperity in the new home, trusting the Union may unflinchingly preserve the stern amateurism and the real tone of the game" (The Morning Post, 1909)

Another notable event that same year was the first home fixture against France. Played close to Twickenham at another location the RFU had considered purchasing – Richmond's Athletic Ground – the match saw Dan Lambert, the Harlequins centre, grab five tries. It is an English record that remains unsurpassed in the twenty-first century. Not bad for a player making his debut.

The first international match held at the new Rugby Football Union Ground (as Twickenham was known long before it became worthy of the lofty title 'Stadium'), saw the greatest team of the period – Wales – make the trip in January 1910 to what was to become the Mecca for English rugby. England had not beaten the team in scarlet since 1898 and yet within the first minute an Adrian Stoop inspired try by Fred Chapman saw England take a lead that they did not relinquish. Wales were on the back foot and that was where they would remain for decades to come. They would have to wait until 1933 for a first victory at the ground.

Scotland's first visit to Twickenham occurred the following season and they managed to get lost in the many allotments still surrounding the former market garden. It was destined to be a particularly unhappy hunting ground for the Scots who would only register four victories at England's headquarters during the entire 20th century.

The new ground was not to everyone's liking, however. Barney Solomon also scored an England try in that opening Twickenham international fixture but then requested that the selectors not pick him again. He claimed that it was too far to travel from his home in Redruth, Cornwall, where he was very content to play for the local club side.

1910 was also the season when France first played a fixture against all of the Home Unions and so hindsight credits it with being the first season of the Five Nations Championship. Until the introduction of the Rugby World Cup competition towards the end of the twentieth century, the Five Nations would remain the world's premier regular rugby contest as well as becoming an integral part of England's social calendar. England won that first ever Five Nations – a title that we have to credit the French press for coining – Tournoi des Cinq Nations. It was England's best season since the great split of 1895.

The aforementioned Adrian Stoop was one of a brilliant crop of new players who had broken through into the England team. Players such as John Birkett, Dan Lambert, 'Cherry' Pilman, and Ronald Poulton (soon to be Poulton-Palmer) rejuvenated the England side and catapulted the

ABOVE Match ticket from Scotland's first visit to Twickenham in 1911

country right back to the top of the European game with a series of wonderful victories that culminated in England's first two Grand Slams - the act of beating all opposition in the Five Nations during a single season.

Stoop was a masterful thinker and the first player to establish different roles for the scrum half and fly half positions, which had previously consisted of two half backs with identical roles standing either side of the scrum. He was also responsible for introducing meticulously planned passing moves to the game. Poulton's play was unashamedly described by all of those fortunate enough to have seen him play as 'genius'. He was an attractive and graceful runner who was able to cross his feet whilst running at full pelt – throwing many an

opposing centre the wrong way. No former Rugby School boy has ever won more international caps.

A January 1913 match against the touring South Africans saw England's first defeat at Twickenham but it also witnessed the debut of two more key players in the seasons to come. WJA 'Dave' Davies and Cyril Lowe completed the side and England would henceforth be untouchable, winning a Grand Slam that year under the captaincy of Norman Wodehouse and then repeating the trick the following season under Poulton.

1913 GRAND SLAM
18 January 1913: **Wales 0 – England 12**, Cardiff Arms Park. *Points scorers – Poulton, Coates, Pillman, Greenwood*

25 January 1913: **England 20 – France 0,** Twickenham. *Points scorers – Coates, Pillman, Poulton, Greenwood*

8 February 1913: **Ireland 4 – England 15,** Lansdowne Road. *Points scorers – Coates, Pillman, Ritson, Greenwood*

15 March 1913: **England 3 – Scotland 0,** Twickenham. *Points scorer – Brown*

ABOVE England team v France 1913: (Back row L-R) Cheesman, Steinthal, Smart, Ritson, Greenwood, Coates, Ward, Davies; (Front row L-R) Brown, Pillman, Poulton, Wodehouse, Johnston, King, Lowe

ABOVE England v France at Twickenham in 1913

During the entire 1913 campaign England scored 13 tries whilst their impregnable defence leaked one solitary drop goal. The victory in Wales was the first Welsh defeat on home soil against another Home Nation since 1898 and it demonstrated rather convincingly that the balance of power had now shifted across the River Severn. Just as notable was the legendary drop goal that Poulton himself scored that day, where the plaudits were quite amazed that he had even managed to get the ball to bounce in a sea of Cardiff mud.

1914 GRAND SLAM

17 January 1914: **England 10 – Wales 9,** Twickenham. *Points scorers – Chapman, Brown, Pillman*

14 February 1914: **England 17 – Ireland 12,** Twickenham. *Points scorers – Lowe, Davies, Pillman, Roberts, Chapman*

21 March 1914: **Scotland 15 – England 16,** Inverleith, Edinburgh. *Points scorers – Lowe, Harrison, Poulton*

---

13 April 1914: **France 13 – England 39,** Stade Colombes, Paris. *Points scorers – Greenwood, Poulton, Lowe, Davies, Watson*

Twenty tries were scored by England in 1914 and Cyril Lowe scored eight of them. When the England team trudged off the pitch after defeating Scotland, however, they were hardly to know that five of them (and six of the Scotland team) were soon to lose their lives in a

far more serious engagement.

Poulton's captaincy of his country was to last a single season. A mere year after leading his side to a Grand Slam one of the finest players to ever wear the white jersey lay dead on the Western Front – killed by a sniper's bullet.

When World War One broke out in 1914 the RFU's attitude was one of total support for the war effort. Within nine days they had sent out a circular to their clubs encouraging all members to join up and fight, which they did, en masse. These amateur sportsmen thought of the War as a great 'away game' and they poured out of the colleges and dressing rooms straight into the army.

It transpired that Rugby's combination of individual strength, teamwork and resilience provided perfect military training. Fearless players on the field became fearless warriors in the trenches and rugby suffered the highest casualty rate of any sport. The statistics from all nations are quite numbing. On the last day of the 1914 season the London Scottish club in Richmond fielded four sides, which equated to 60 men. Only 15 of those 60 players would return home from the war.

ENGLAND INTERNATIONAL PLAYERS
WHO DIED IN THE FIRST WORLD WAR

LEFT Lest We Forget

Name	Caps	Age
H Alexander	7 (1900-02)	36
H Berry	4 (1910)	32
A J Dingle	3 (1913-14)	23
G E B Dobbs	2 (1906)	32
L Haigh	7 (1910-11)	35
R H M Hands	2 (1910)	29
A L Harrison	2 (1914)	32
H A Hodges	2 (1906)	32
R E Inglis	3 (1886)	53
P D Kendall	3 (1901-03)	37
J A King	12 (1911-13)	32
R O Lagden	1 (1911)	25
D Lambert	7 (1907-11)	32
A F Maynard	3 (1914)	22
E R Mobbs	7 (1909-10)	35
W M B Nanson	2 (1907)	34
F E Oakeley	4 (1913-14)	23
R L Pillman	1 (1914)	23
R W Poulton-Palmer	17 (1909-14)	25
J E Raphael	9 (1902-06)	35
R O Schwarz	3 (1899-01)	43
L A N Slocock	8 (1907-08)	29
F N Tarr	4 (1909-13)	27
A F Todd	2 (1900)	31
J H D Watson	3 (1914)	24
A J Wilson	1 (1909)	30
C E Wilson	1 (1898)	43

1920-1939

Heady Days

"Rugby is a game of beauty and power"
William Wakefield, England captain

THE FULL HORROR OF THE FIRST
World War was not immediately
revealed following its bloody conclusion
and so rugby happily continued to asso-
ciate itself with the 'glorious effort'.
Professional soccer had not ceased during the War and so rugby felt justified in
taking and holding the moral high
ground due to the game's commitment
to the conflict. This even extended, in a
quite disturbing way, to using rugby's
war dead as justification for the continuing battle against professionalism.
Whenever the concept of professionalism in the union game was proposed,
usually from Australia where union was
fighting a rearguard action against mass
interest in rugby league and Aussie
Rules, the proponent shot down in

RIGHT MacIlwaine
(seated left) had last
played for England in
1912 and is surrounded
by new players and
their new jersey
badges, 1920

flames. Dyed-in-the-wool amateurs
expressed revulsion that the idea was
even being entertained since it was felt
to be highly disrespectful to those amateur players who had given their lives
during the slaughter.

The great losses meant that with the
resumption of international rugby in
1920 there were wholesale changes in
the composition of the England side
and 11 of the 15 who ran out at Swansea
to face Wales were new caps. Until now
it was the practice for players to not
only supply their own white jersey

(which was used repeatedly) but to also have a red rose of their own design embroidered on to the left breast. However, so many new players requiring jerseys created the opportunity for a first standardised rose. Alf Wright, an RFU's clerk designed a rose which was subsequently placed on to every new England jersey until the very tail end of the twentieth century.

It is highly unlikely that it was inspired by pride in their new sartorial elegance, but the 1920s was a phenomenally successful decade for English rugby, on and off the pitch. The strength of the pre-war Grand Slam winning side was maintained, despite the horrendous loses, thanks to the introduction of new players who were more than capable of holding their own in the international arena.

On the pitch William Wakefield came to symbolise the decade. Wakefield was a loose forward of impeccable credentials, movie-star good looks, and was a remarkable captain. According to legend he didn't feel that a game had actually started until he had received at least one punch to the face. He could play almost anywhere in the forward pack and even turned out as a centre for his club, Harlequins. Wakefield turned the back row forward into a powerful, mobile defensive tool and was also a great thinker and student of the game who wrote extensively on techniques and tactics. He was obsessed, for example, with the fact that a player running at full pelt would momentarily increase his speed when stumbling. How could that latent extra speed be harnessed?

Wakefield played 31 times for England (including a run of 29 consecutive matches) and remained the country's most capped player until the mid 1970s. His profile in the game continued as an RFU administrator after hanging up his boots, and was also as a Member of Parliament.

The great shadow that Wakefield threw over the decade has actually allowed another potential England legend to all but disappear from view. 'Dave' Davies had featured in both pre-war Grand Slams at fly half and continued to play for England through the first half of

BELOW William Wakefield

ABOVE England team v Wales 1921: (Back row L-R) Gardner, Woods, Myers, Voyce, Blackiston, Smallwood, Mellish, Cumberledge; (Middle row L-R) Hammett, Edwards, Brown, Davies, Lowe, Wakefield; (Front row) Kershaw

the 1920s. An England selector once described him as "the greatest match-winner who ever put on a football boot" and it is regrettable that this remarkable player has been overlooked in comparison to his contemporaries. The cynical might wonder if it was because he was born in Wales.

Davies was destined to captain two Grand Slam winning sides to Wakefield's one, play in four Grand Slam winning sides to Wakefield's three and following the defeat against South Africa on his debut he never featured in another England loss. An incredible record of 20 victories and one draw in international matches followed in a career that, interrupted by the War,

lasted for a decade.

The very first player to feature in every single match of four Grand Slam winning seasons was Cyril Lowe, upon whose wartime exploits as a RAF pilot the fictional character of 'Biggles' was supposedly based and whose England try scoring record was to stand for 57 years. Lowe was immortalised in verse by Jeeves and Wooster creator PG Wodehouse who would watch him out on the wing, awaiting the ball: "There he stood, poor little chappie, looking lonely and unhappy".

1921 GRAND SLAM

15 January 1921: **England 18 – Wales 3,** Twickenham. *Points scorers – Smallwood, Davies, Kershaw, Lowe, Hammett*

12 February 1921: **England 15 – Ireland 0,** Twickenham. *Points scorers – Lowe, Blackiston, Brown, Cumberlege*

19 March 1921: **Scotland 0 – England 18,** Inverleith, Edinburgh. *Points scorers – Hammett, Brown, Edwards, King, Woods*

28 March 1921: **France 6 – England 10,** Stade Colombes, Paris. *Points scorers – Hammett, Blakiston, Lowe*

The new crop of England players also included Cyril Kershaw, who formed a legendary half-back partnership with Davies that recorded a wins-to-results ratio that will seldom be bettered: played 14 together, won 13, drawn one. Tom Voyce (great uncle of the 21st century England player of the same name), Arthur Blackiston and Dr Ronald Cove-Smith featured amongst Davies' phenomenal forwards. The 1922 season also featured the single appearance of the improbably and incredibly named Peveril Barton Reibey Wallop William-Powlett (later Vice Admiral, Sir Peveril Barton etc…). One suspects that he was never a target of the Northern Union.

That Davies was not in the side for his team's defeat in Cardiff in 1922 may have had as much to do with the subsequent defeat as the waterlogged pitch that had been saturated by a week of uninterrupted rain. It was one of only two defeats that England endured at the hands of the other Home Unions between 1912 and 1925.

1923 GRAND SLAM

20 January 1923: **England 7 – Wales 3,** Twickenham. *Points scorers – Smallwood, Price*

10 February 1923: **England 23 – Ireland 5,** Welford Road, Leicester. *Points scorers – Conway, Davies, Corbett, Lowe, Price, Smallwood, Voyce*

17 March 1923: **Scotland 6 – England 8,** Inverleith, Edinburgh. *Points scorers – Smallwood, Voyce, Luddington*

2 April 1923: **France 3 – England 12,** Stade Colombes, Paris. *Points scorers – Davies, Conway, Wakefield, Luddington*

ABOVE England team v Wales 1923: (Back row L-R) Smallwood, Edwards, Price, Cove-Smith, Voyce, Myres; (Middle row L-R) Gardner, Kershaw, Lowe, Davies, Wakefield, Corbett, Gilbert; (Front row L-R) Conway, Luddington

ABOVE WJA 'Dave' Davies

Leicester's Welford Road ground was chosen in 1923 to see what the reaction would be if occasional England home games were taken back out into the provinces. A major victory was secured against Ireland, but a lower than expected crowd of 20,000 put paid to that particular initiative. The next England home game away from Twickenham would not come until the rebuilding of Headquarters necessitated the use of Wembley Stadium against Canada in 1992.

A fourth Grand Slam in six seasons had done nothing to harm the popularity of the game in England. The 1920s saw an explosion in the playing of rugby in English schools as soccer suffered from increasing identification with professionalism and bad sportsmanship. There was a huge rise in the number of Grammar Schools and rugby football was seen as an easy way of aping the traditional Public School trappings and ethics to which the Grammar Schools aspired.

As the new Grammar schools copied public school traditions such as forming 'houses', wearing symbolic blazers, caps, ties and badges, England players such as Wakefield served as the all-round Boy's Own heroes who strengthened the game's hold on the public imagination. Old Boys rugby clubs from these new schools clubs took the name of their former school, rather than their locality and more new clubs were formed in England in the 1920s than in any other decade. Rugby had found itself a new role and a very definable image. The trauma of the 1895 split was being shaken off, both on and off the pitch. By the end of the twentieth century the two English counties containing the most RFU clubs would be Middlesex and …'rebellious' Yorkshire.

Wakefield took over the England captaincy following Davies' retirement in 1923. That Kershaw and Lowe also retired at the same time could have caused a lesser side to stumble, but it only served to make Wakefield's 1924 Grand Slam even more impressive.

ABOVE Some of the England team v Wales, 1924: (L-R) Young, Chantrill, Robson, Conway, Voyce, Wakefield, Cove-Smith, Luddington

1924 GRAND SLAM

19 January 1924: **Wales 9 – England 17**, St Helens, Swansea. *Points scorers – Catcheside, Jacob, Locke, Myers, Conway*

9 February 1924: **Ireland 3 – England 14**, Ravenhill, Belfast. *Points scorers – Catcheside, Corbett, Hamilton-Wickes, Conway*

23 February 1924: **England 19 – France 7**, Twickenham. *Points scorers – Jacob, Conway, Catcheside, Young*

15 March 1924: **England 19 – Scotland 0**, Twickenham. *Points scorers – Myers, Conway, Catcheside, Wakefield*

Carston Catcheside, Cyril Lowe's replacement on the wing, scored a try in each match of the 1924 Five Nations campaign and remained the only Englishman during the entire history of the Five Nations to achieve the feat.

England had now won 33 out of 41 matches since the opening of Twickenham in 1910, but cracks were beginning to show in the ageing squad. New Zealand returned to the British Isles in 1924, keen to improve on the almost spotless record of their 1905 predecessors. Despite having Cyril Brownlie sent off at Twickenham (the first international sending off in history after only 10 minutes for kicking an

England player lying on the ground) the All Blacks went on to win 11-17. These New Zealanders would earn their 'Invincibles' nickname by winning every game of their 29 match tour of the British Isles.

England's unbeaten run in the Five Nations dating back three seasons was also undone. The location was Edinburgh and the occasion was the opening of Scotland's new national stadium, Murrayfield. The Scots prevailed in a match that Wakefield was to describe as "an exceedingly hard game… I felt the effects of it for several days afterwards". 70,000 lucky souls gained entry into the ground and saw Scotland win their first ever Grand Slam. Only two seasons before the equivalent fixture had been watched by 30,000.

Two more unwanted landmarks were achieved in the following two seasons. 1926 witnessed the first defeat at Twickenham against a Home Union side as Scotland triumphed 17-9. The following year the England team was beaten by France for the very first time. Unfortunately the match also happened to be Wakefield's last for his country and it was an entirely inappropriate stage for such a great player to step down. His last

RIGHT The radio commentator's box at Twickenham, 1927

BELOW Carston Catcheside

F. & J. SMITH'S CIGARETTES.

H. C. CATCHESIDE.
(PERCY PARK & ENGLAND.)

season also witnessed the first appearance at Twickenham of a brand new concept that was destined to take English rugby into millions of homes - the very first radio match commentary.

The last remaining member of Wakefield's 1924 Grand Slam pack was Cove-Smith and he was elevated to captain. Although his was by no means a vintage side they did manage something new. Not only was another Grand Slam achieved – the fourth of the decade – but Cove-Smith's side became the first to achieve that success and also defeat an international touring side in the same season. New South Wales were the victims and they were given the status of an international side because the only other rugby-playing Australian state (Queensland) had withdrawn from the game as rugby league continued to consume the east coast of that nation.

1928 GRAND SLAM

21 January 1928: **Wales 8 – England 10**, St Helens, Swansea. *Points scorers – Richardson, Laird, Taylor*

11 February 1928: **Ireland 6 – England 7,** Lansdowne Road, Dublin. *Points scorers – Richardson*

25 February 1928: **England 18 – France 8**, Twickenham. *Points scorers – Palmer, Periton, Richardson*

17 March 1928: **England 6 – Scotland 0**, Twickenham. *Points scorers – Hanley, Laird*

The success was England's sixth Grand Slam in eleven seasons. It was an incredible sequence and a period of domination to match the great Welsh

teams of the 1970s, both statistically and psychologically.

Cove-Smith had matched Davies and Lowe in playing in four Grand Slam sides. Following Cove-Smith's retirement in 1929, the next England player to achieve the feat would be Jason Leonard. These four players, along with Frenchmen Fabien Pelous and Olivier Magne, remain the only ones from any nation to have achieved done so. However, Lowe remains unique in having played every second of every single match in four Grand Slam seasons.

ABOVE England team v France 1928: (Back row L-R) Stark, Taylor, Richardson, Aarvold, Hanley, Prentice, Palmer; (Middle row L-R) Sparks, Stanbury, Cove-Smith, Tucker, Periton, Sellar (Front row L-R) Laird, Young

In the 1920s Wales, the once all-powerful side in the British Isles, managed to win a mere seven of the 26 matches that they played after narrowly missing out on a Grand Slam in 1922. All of Britain was suffering from the effects of a worldwide economic depression but, with many of Wales' better players being manual workers, financial security was precarious and they were far more susceptible to the overtures of the rugby league clubs who could offer them the pay packet that union would not allow. The effect was always magnified if their national side was struggling on the pitch.

The disparity between the effect on Wales and England can be seen in the numbers who were tempted 'North'. Wales were destined to lose 158 international players to rugby league, whilst England lost only 51, a fair portion of who moved across immediately after the 1895 split. The generally more affluent and financially stable playing population of England was far less likely to be lured to Wakefield or Warrington than their Welsh counterparts and it is fascinating to consider just how dominant Wales might have been over the decades were it not for this almost constant player-drain.

Whilst England remained competitive through the 1930s they were also inconsistent. In fact the only aspect that remained unchanged throughout the decade (and beyond) were the dark blue socks with white top that were introduced half way through the 1930 season to replace the club socks that players had previously worn.

Inconsistency on the pitch was not helped by increasingly eccentric selection policies, as it dawned on those in charge that replacements for the magnificent players of the early 1920s had not come through. Defeat at the hands of France in 1931 consigned England to the bottom of the table and ownership of the 'wooden spoon' for the first time in the Five Nations era. Opportunity for revenge in 1932 was denied, however, because France was expelled from the Championship. This was hard on England captains Bernard Gadney and Tuppy Owen-Smith since England won all of their matches in 1934 under the former and in 1937 under the later. France's absence removed their opportunity to go for a Grand Slam and join the pantheon of great England captains.

The reason given for the French expulsion was the "unsatisfactory con-

dition of the game of Rugby Football as managed and played in France" which actually meant the off field professionalism and on field violence in their club game. During the years immediately before the banishment there were three high profile on-pitch deaths in major French club matches, whilst certain club owners blatantly and unashamedly offered payments to tempt the best players to their clubs. Advertisements from French clubs looking for players

The Home Unions suspended all contact until the French could get their house in order.

It was a situation that merely confirmed to the RFU that no good could come from club competition and they happily watched on as English clubs jostled with each other for friendly fixtures. Club games would provide nothing more sinister than a fun match and, presuming that the right fixtures could be obtained, improved social standing. A French return was earmarked for the 1939/40 season but this was delayed due to the outbreak of World War Two.

The period following Wakefield's retirement saw less innovation on the pitch. The play of the era is well summed up by former England player Dai Gent in this instruction to forwards in his 1933 book 'Rugby Football': "Handling the ball is only a minor part of your job, so don't give much thought to it".

The greatest game of the decade was to give England captain Gadney the opportunity for immortality that the French absence might otherwise have denied him. Saturday 4 January 1936 was the first time that the All Blacks ever

could even be spotted in British regional newspapers! The situation reached a (political) head when ten French clubs tried to set up their own Federation.

lost on English soil, having successfully negotiated 57 previous encounters with English clubs, counties and the national side without suffering so much as a draw. 72,000 supporters crammed into Twickenham to see Russian-born Prince Alexander Obolensky score two remarkable solo tries on his England debut, the second of which saw him cut diagonally across the pitch. Hal Sever on the other England wing also scored on his debut and on any other day Sever

would have been the hero. Sever's moment in the spotlight came the following season when he scored vital points in all of England's victories under new captain Owen-Smith.

Pathe News screenings of Obolensky's two tries in film theatres across the country made him a national hero and helped to cement Twickenham's place firmly in the public consciousness. The headquarters of the union game was moving from being a rugby venue to becoming a national icon, a process that gained momentum in 1938 when the match against Scotland at Twickenham was the first ever televised live - a six try thriller that ended 16-21 in Scotland's favour.

Obolensky was destined to win only three more caps for his adopted country. On 29 March 1940, aged just 24, he crashed whilst piloting a Hurricane fighter plane. He was to be the first England player to lose his life during the Second World War.

ABOVE Prince Alexander Obolensky playing for Rosslyn Park

LEFT Obolensky training with the RAF

Shuffled to the bottom of the pack

"The only place for a coach in rugby is for transporting the teams to the match."
Eric Evans, England captain

WHILST EVERY DEATH IN WAR IS tragic it is particularly cruel that Norman Wodehouse's name sits on the Second World War list. England's first ever Grand Slam captain, back in 1913, had survived the entire First World War, risen to the rank of Rear Admiral in the Royal Navy and then been recalled from retirement for the Second World War, aged 54. He drowned at sea whilst commanding a convoy in the Atlantic.

During the war the RFU temporarily revoked their professionalism laws, as they had done in the Great War, and permitted union and league servicemen to play together on the same pitch. A series of wartime international matches were followed by Victory Internationals in 1946. In total, 24 matches were played by 'England' sides but caps were never awarded and the games not granted official status since the strongest possible side was not available.

The new era saw the return of France into the international fold. They had been invited back in 1939, under pressure from the British government who were desperate to tighten all bonds with

ENGLAND INTERNATIONAL PLAYERS
WHO DIED IN THE SECOND WORLD WAR

LEFT 1944 Wartime match programme

Name	Caps	Age
B H Black	10 (1930-33)	23
L A Booth	7 (1933-35)	33
P Cooke	2 (1939)	23
V G Davies	2 (1922-25)	42
H D Freakes	3 (1938-39)	28
R A Gerrard	14 (1932-36)	30
W G E Luddington	13 (1923-26)	46
R M Marshall	5 (1938-39)	27
A Obolensky	4 (1936)	24
E I Parsons	1 (1939)	27
H Rew	10 (1929-34)	24
C C Tanner	5 (1930-32)	22
D E Teden	3 (1939)	24
N A Wodehouse	14 (1910-13)	54

France as Europe slipped towards war. Parliamentary leverage had even included the offer of using Royal influence to rearrange fixtures between the unions but the outbreak of hostilities had prevented any French return until 1947. Anyone who ever suggests that sport and politics do not mix need only take a cursory glance at the history of rugby union to see that the areas actually fit together like a hand in a perfectly tailored glove. Meanwhile professionalism continued to run rife in France, as admitted by various British players who joined French clubs over subsequent years.

The first match of the post war era was against Wales in 1947 and 14 new England players were awarded caps, eight of whom were still students. That Championship was shared with Wales but then England were to win only four of their next 19 games.

The Twickenham ground had been

ABOVE Twickenham being used as a service depot during World War II

witnessed a defeat at the hands of Wales. The England team were to end up at the bottom of the Five Nations pile in 1948, 1950 and 1951. These (and 1931) were the only four occasions that England was to suffer receipt of the wooden spoon between 1910 and 1966.

Player selection was assisted for many years by three official trial matches, where new and upcoming talent was assessed. Although the pattern altered over the decades these generally kicked off with a Whites v Colours match in the autumn, played at a small club ground. Probables v Possibles was held straight after the Oxford v Cambridge Varsity match, which was itself seen as an unofficial trial, and was held at a larger club ground. The third trial match was held at Twickenham in January and was billed as either England v The Rest or the Final Trial.

As Peter Jackson, an England great of the period, remembers, "In the early 1950s, the England team was always

used as a service depot and suffered a slight amount of bomb damage during the War but in 1950 an official Twickenham crowd of 75,532 packed into the stands and onto the terraces. It was a record attendance that would not be bettered until the completion of the modern, three-tiered bowl in the early 21st century. Sadly, and yet unsurprisingly for the period, the record crowd

ABOVE Twickenham's record crowd see Wales score a try in 1950

being chopped and changed. The selectors took far too much notice of the latest crop of players from Oxford and Cambridge Universities. For the whole of their autumn term those players trained and played like professionals. So just for those three months they were fitter than they would ever be again in their lives. Very few of them lasted"

Radio and television coverage might have started to popularise the game outside rugby circles but the players themselves were still a long way from being treated as important assets by their own governing body. It was the administrators who held the power and the players were merely expendable cannon fodder in constant fear of de-selection following a slightly below-par performance. Nowhere is this better exemplified than

ABOVE The 1952 Oxford University v Cambridge University 'Varsity' match at Twickenham

in OL Owen's 1955 book, 'History of the Rugby Football Union'. The tome contains 67 photographic images, yet only one solitary picture features England rugby players, and then it is a photograph of the very first side from way back in 1871. The vast majority of images depict various RFU Presidents, Secretaries and Committees. There was no mistaking where the Union's priorities lay.

As the 1950s progressed, improvements on the pitch saw the England team fall only one win short of Grand Slams in successive years after failing to defeat Wales (1952), Ireland (1953) and France (1954). The 1954 England v Wales match at Twickenham was the very first 'all ticket' affair at the Stadium, demonstrating that support for the international game was continuing to grow.

The early 1950s even saw the commencement of the longest period that England was to ever hold the Calcutta Cup. It would be 13 seasons before it was relinquished to Scotland.

For the first game of the 1956 season ten new players were awarded England caps, eight of whom would play in every game of the following season's Grand Slam. The selectors, whether through blind panic or incredible foresight, had managed to assemble the best England side since the 1920s.

The new players included Peter Jackson, the elusive runner from Coventry; Dickie Jeeps, the scrum half who had been overlooked at an England trial six years before, but came to prominence following a wonderful 1955 Lions tour to New Zealand; Ron Jacobs the powerful prop; and Marques and Currie, a pair of locks who would make 22 consecutive appearances together.

ABOVE Eric Evans walks from the field, 1956

The new players blended in perfectly with existing stalwarts such as Eric Evans, a natural leader of men who took over the captaincy in 1956. The Sale hooker was a fitness fanatic who trained

with Manchester United's professional soccer players. Jeff Butterfield was another fitness-obsessive and played for the top English club of the time, Northampton. The third great England team had been assembled. Although the match against Wales was lost they would only lose two of their next 20 fixtures in a sequence that took them into the 1960s.

The 1957 Grand Slam season started in Wales, as was typical at the time with matches still being played in a traditional sequence, rather than on a revolving rota.

1957 GRAND SLAM

19 January 1957: **Wales 0 – England 3,** Cardiff Arms Park. *Points scorer – Allison*

9 February 1957: **Ireland 0 – England 6,** Lansdowne Road, Dublin. *Points scorers – Challis, Jackson*

23 February 1957: **England 9 – France 5,** Twickenham. *Points scorers – Jackson, Evans*

16 March 1957: **England 16 – Scotland 3**, Twickenham. *Points scorers – Challis, Davies, Higgins, Thompson*

Eric Evans' 1957 success brought about the first printed reference to the 'Grand Slam' phrase in a rugby context when The Times and The Telegraph used the expression when reporting upon the adventures of the Sale man's team. Evans would captain England a record equalling 13 occasions. Subsequent captains Dickie Jeeps and John Pullin would also reach 13, but the record would not be bettered until Bill Beaumont's turn at the helm in the early 1980s.

The following season's hard fought victory over Australia was a particularly rough battle that saw the England casualties pile up. Jeff Butterfield was knocked out four times, Hetherington was concussed and after 30 minutes Phil Horrocks-Taylor was forced to retire from the game injured. When an Australian player stamped on Peter Thompson the crowd disquiet gave way to mass booing – the very first time that such an event was witnessed at a Twickenham international.

OPPOSITE England team 1957 v France: (Back row L-R) Butterfield, Davies, Thompson, Marques, Currie, Robbins, Jacobs, Challis; (Middle row L-R) Jackson, Hastings, Evans, Ashcroft, Higgins; (Front row L-R) Bartlett, Jeeps

LEFT Hetherington is helped from the pitch following England v Australia, 1958

Rather worryingly, the 1957 Grand Slam was to be England's only such highlight between 1928 and 1980 – an incredible length of time for the game's founding nation to suffer. The fracturing of the 1957 team signalled the beginning of a terrible trough – the worst and longest that England has ever suffered. The victories began to dry up once Evans stepped down and the side crumbled almost as quickly as it had gelled. A Triple Crown success in 1960 under the captaincy of Jeeps would also

prove to be the last until 1980.

Not only were victories in short supply, but the nature of the game itself was far from spectacular. In 1959 England managed to register a grand total of nine points during their entire Five Nations campaign - yet still avoided coming bottom of the table! This was not the era to be sitting in the stands if you wanted to marvel at open, end to end contests and free-scoring wingers. The wonderful rugby played by the 1955 and 1959 British Isles touring sides suggested that all was well in the British game, when it was blatantly far from well. The only Five Nations side playing with any real zest at the time were the French. It was the period when they first rose to pre-eminence in Europe, their first outright Five Nations title being won in 1959.

As the 1960s arrived it started to seem as though a real nadir in the British game had been reached. In January 1962 England and Wales slogged out a 0-0 draw, destined (hopefully) to be the last ever seen at Twickenham. The dominant tactics of the period were derived from the '10 man' rugby which was used to great effect by the Springboks on their 1931 tour of the British Isles.

BELOW French supporters on the Twickenham pitch in 1959

Forwards would battle for possession of the ball and move it back to their fly half who, at the time, was allowed to kick directly into touch from anywhere on the pitch. The forwards would then trundle forward and repeat the same tactic again and again. It meant lots of possession and very little back play. The style was widely copied and would be seen at its very worst during the notorious Scotland v Wales game of 1965 which featured 111 line outs - a line out every 43 seconds.

Not only was the domestic international tournament shockingly dull but, as the decade proceeded, successive Lions sides would be thrashed by South Africa and New Zealand, whose own touring sides to these Isles were almost untouchable. What a perfect time then for the England team to undertake their first ever foreign tour!

ABOVE Wales miss a kick in Twickenham's last international 0-0 draw, 1962

In a Dragon's shadow

"We may not be much good, but at least we turn up"
John Pullin, England captain, 1973

THE BOOM IN AIR TRAVEL MEANT that there was now an alternative to spending endless weeks on a ship and it enabled the first England oversees tour to take place in 1963. Scotland had been the first Home Nation to undertake such a tour, three years previously, whilst the first Lions side to travel by aeroplane had been the party who flew to South Africa in 1955. Three test defeats in the space of eleven days (two against New Zealand and one in Australia) saw England return home empty handed. Colin Meads, the legendary All Black forward famously described the English forwards of the period as having "too many sweat bands and not enough sweat".

If anything had been learned from

the experiences of 1963's short tour it did not reveal itself immediately. England would only win two games during the following three seasons. Far more important was the fact that a 'flying' visit by a test team was now entirely possible. Tours would become shorter and the Southern Hemisphere nations began to campaign for the creation of a world championship for the game.

The Rugby World Cup tournament was still a few decades away from realisation and in the meantime the unofficial world championship would remain the occasional clashes between New Zealand and South Africa. Tours by both of these nations to the British Isles also increased during the 1960s as the All Blacks pioneered a style of all-out attacking, handling, 15-man rugby.

England did not have to look across to the other side of the world to find a nemesis, however. There was a much more serious problem just over the River Severn. England won at Cardiff in 1963 but it would prove to be their last

victory in Wales for an astonishing 28 years. Out of the 16 seasons that followed 1963 Wales finished below England only twice in the Five Nations table. On those two occasions, when England was statistically a more successful side, fate saw to it that they actually failed to beat the men in scarlet, so were denied the opportunity to enjoy their higher ranking. In this period England won only 23 of 81 matches,

ABOVE England losing in Cardiff, 1965

OPPOSITE England players training at Twickenham in 1963 prior to their first overseas tour

ABOVE England v Ireland 1966 - Dave Powell gets familiar with the East Stand

changing and recalling with no semblance of continuity. A defeat would lead to the dismissal of any number of experienced players, the selectors fiddling with combinations to resolve perceived problems in the team. England's selectors may not have had the modern advantages of access to video footage, live television matches or a league structure that allowed them to watch the best clubs, but then neither did the other Home Unions.

In 1965 Andy Hancock's incredible 90 metre run against Scotland in the dying seconds at Twickenham prevented a first Scottish victory on English soil since 1938. The conversion might have been missed but defeat was averted and the game was drawn 3-3. Hancock's reward would be English rugby immortality, but in the short term he was forced to endure a year long wait for his next England cap while the selectors kept on fiddling.

Luck was also conspicuous by its absence during the era. In 1967 England travelled to Cardiff and scored more points than ever before on Welsh soil; and still lost 34-21.

Changes were taking place, however,

losing 50. The 1960s and 1970s were dismal decades for England.

The finger of blame was often pointed at the country's very haphazard selection policy and it is easy to see why. There was constant player chopping,

that would shape the modern game. In 1969 the IRFB responded to the 10-man kicking game by altering the rules so that the ball could only be kicked directly into touch from within the 25 yard line. In the same year England assembled their players together for a month under their first ever coach, former Northampton flanker Don White. The first replacements for injuries were also allowed and England's first was Tim Dalton. Typically for the period Dalton never played for his country again.

The new era got off to a flying start with a first ever win over South Africa at a Twickenham fixture marred by anti-apartheid demonstrations. Some demonstrators rubbed acid into the face of the police who were trying to keep them off the playing surface and sections of the crowd, encouraged to take actions into their own hands by the Twickenham tannoy announcer, helped police to clear

ABOVE Don White (left) training the England forwards, 1971

the pitch. The Springboks would not visit again until 1992, after their racist apartheid policies had been repealed.

The almost universal sporting boycott of South African was not entirely shared by rugby. England toured there in 1972 and 1984 and the reason was that old chestnut amateurism. Concerned that total isolation would encourage large

ABOVE Anti-apartheid demonstrators march on Twickenham

into the wound Scotland also won their first match at Twickenham since 1938.

A 1972 tour to South Africa took place when the England team were at their lowest ever ebb. After just one victory in the previous 13 tests they faced a South African side that had never lost at home to any of the Home Unions. The result was a remarkable 9-18 victory to England, thanks to Sam Doble's kicks and Alan Morley's try. The tour itself witnessed seven England victories and one draw. It was a quite remarkable and entirely unexpected haul.

There is no doubt at all that quality players were available at the time. Coventry's David Duckham had a wonderful centre partnership with Headingley's John Spencer which lasted for all of nine matches until the selectors moved Duckham out to the wing. Duckham, quite aware of this waste of his talent, dryly noted that "I didn't receive another pass for about two years".

John Pullin was another England great of the era and somehow managed to string together a remarkable 36 match run that would see him play every second of every match until Jan 1975. Duckham and Pullin starred in

South African businesses to sponsor professional incoming tours, the rugby community kept South African rugby close and never expelled them from the IRFB. However, exclusion from the first two Rugby World Cup tournaments would tear South African rugby apart and at the very least made them mindful of the need for change.

The very depths were plumbed, ironically enough, just after the RFU celebrated its centenary in 1971. The England team was 'white-washed' (defeated in every match of the Five Nations) for the only two times in its history in 1972 and 1976. To rub salt

the famous 1973 Barbarians v New Zealand match at the Arms Park in Cardiff, one of the greatest exhibitions of running rugby ever seen. These players alongside Peter Dixon, Fran Cotton and Roger Uttley also shone on the superb British Isles tours of 1971 and 1974 where they were essential ingredients of the mix.

So what was wrong? It seemed that the step up from the regular diet of friendly club fixtures to international fixtures, with no stepping stone other than the County Championship in

BELOW John Spencer passes to David Duckham in Cardiff, 1969

ABOVE John Pullin

were honed in their own club championship. It was still too big a jump for the RFU to take, however. They could not face the idea of regular, competitive club rugby, scared as always that amateurism would tumble. They bowed to pressure and introduced a first ever national knock-out cup competition in 1972 and players and clubs at last had something other than pride to play for in occasional matches, but it was still not enough.

Ironically the outstanding European club of the era - supplying seven players to the sublime 1971 British Isles touring side - was based in London only a few punts away from Twickenham. The pity was that it was London Welsh and their success would have nothing but a detrimental effect on England's efforts. As a Welsh supporter quipped to an England selector after yet another defeat in Cardiff: "Never mind, you had the nicest jerseys".

1973's match against Ireland at Lansdowne Road was particularly significant, but not because of the on-pitch action. Wales and Scotland had refused to play in Dublin the previous season following an overspill of sectarian violence from Northern Ireland to Dublin, that had seen the British embassy

between, was just too great. In 1973 the Scots started a league competition for their clubs and the talents of the great French players of the period, the only genuine rivals to Wales in the 1970s,

attacked. England gained a rapturous standing ovation upon taking to the pitch, but then lost. "We may not be much good, but at least we turn up" declared captain, John Pullin, at the post match dinner.

The unstable political situation in another part of the world was responsible for a second match that was to enter English rugby folklore. Concerned about the political situation in Argentina and associated kidnapping threats, a 1973 England tour was cancelled and replaced with a last minute trip to Fiji and New Zealand. Having failed to string together three successive victories for 15 years, very little was expected of the England team, especially after defeats against every New Zealand provincial side they faced at the start of the tour. The 16-10 victory over the All Blacks, inspired by Moseley fly half Jan Webster, was to remain England's only victory on New Zealand soil until 2003.

Upon returning home Australia were beaten 20-3 at Twickenham and, incredibly, the worst England team in history had triumphed over all three major Southern Hemisphere sides within 18 months. In 1974 they recorded their

only Twickenham victory over Wales between 1963 and 1980, but there was to be no great celebration. Everyone connected with the game was still mourning the resultant loss of life when an aeroplane crash killed supporters returning from an England match in Paris.

The 1970s saw a rise in Welsh and Scottish nationalism that led to increasingly unpleasant atmospheres in the grounds of both countries when England visited. Long gone were the days when a vanquished team would carry off the victorious opposition captain on their shoulders.

As if the on-pitch trials and tribulations were not enough, the popularity of the game off the field again conspired to strain the RFU to the full. The first live television coverage of a game at Twickenham had occurred in the late 1930s, but mud-caked players in similarly designed kits were never likely to win a ratings war on black and white

ABOVE The 1973 tour to Argentina was cancelled so late in the day that the blazer badges had already been produced

television sets. The flair, finesse and success of the Welsh and Lions sides of the 1970s coincided with the explosion of colour television in Britain. Unprecedented publicity for the 15 man game brought attention from many new quarters.

Mike Burton was to make a name for himself in 1975 as the first English player to be sent off in an international match, following a 4th minute tackle on an Australian in Brisbane. However, he

BELOW Michael O'Brien streaking at Twickenham in 1974. Note the lack of any pitch side advertising

is better known for his exposure of the 'boot money' scams that were rife in the 'shamateur' days. He recalls that he was paid £50 (and a free pair of boots) to wear Adidas products in an international fixture. On the match day in question all 15 England players were wearing the same boots and so the company had in effect managed to buy itself an 80 minute television advertisement in front of millions of people for only £750. There was even an occasion when England forward Andy Ripley wore a different make of boot on each foot to please two companies.

The RFU ordered the players to paint out the white Adidas stripes, but the episode merely indicated the direction that increased media interest was going to take the game. Whether the Union liked it or not their game was now in the public eye and subject to associated commercial pressures. During the 1960s the only sponsorship deemed acceptable to the RFU had been that used to assist in the making of rugby training and coaching films in strict co-operation with the Union. Blatant commercial sponsorship was "contrary to amateur principles".

However, in 1972 the IRFB decreed

that 'financial assistance' (i.e. sponsorship) was permissible under certain strict guidelines. Advertising within Twickenham Stadium, which had first been mooted in the 1950s, was also now deemed possible - if exercised with due discretion. The first perimeter signage appeared in January 1974. In 1975 John Player Special took on the sponsorship of the RFU's knock out cup competition and they were to be followed in later decades by Pilkington, Tetley and Powergen.

Extra revenue was coming into the game but so were extra pressures, such as the increased demands that coaches were placing on the amateur players who also had to balance their extra training sessions with family commitments and jobs. As Margaret Thatcher's Conservative Party came into power in 1979 they ushered in a period of self-motivation and a creed of 'what's in it for me?' Amateurism for the rugby union authorities was about more than being

paid for playing. It was also an ethos that embodied good sportsmanship, gentlemanly behaviour, self restraint and character building and the fear was that professionalism would eat into those qualities. How much longer could the game stay amateur under these combined pressures?

ABOVE Peter Dixon, John Scott, Bill Beaumont and others training prior to a match with the USA in 1977

Another false dawn?

"All the press, who had written millions of cutting, damning words about English rugby between 1957 and 1980,…could only guess what that moment of ecstasy actually felt like"
Bill Beaumont, England captain, 1982

A FAR MORE SETTLED SELECTION policy, improved coaching under new trainer Mike Davies and the creation of the RFU's cup competition for clubs were all contributory factors in reversing the 1970s slump. In 1979 former England captain Budge Rogers became chairman of selectors. He consulted closely with his captain, Bill Beaumont, and held a more steadfast approach to selection which also benefited the side.

The 1980 Grand Slam under Bill Beaumont was a superb triumph in a period of mediocrity. That most of the pieces of the jigsaw had been available for about five years only highlighted the talent that the selection policy had con-

trived to squander. The playing mix included experienced players such as Fran Cotton, the fearsome prop forward, and Dusty Hare, the point machine at full back. They combined with young talents such as Clive Woodward at centre, who came in to replace Tony Bond after the latter broke his leg early in the 1980 campaign. England were assisted no little that season by Wales' Paul Ringer, whose assault on John Horton won him a sending off, a few minutes into the first game, helping England to a precious narrow victory. Subsequently Woodward was to inspire a demolition of Scotland that included a hat trick of tries from John

RIGHT Clive Woodward

Carlton (England's first since 1924) and a Grand Slam for Bill Beaumont.

1980 GRAND SLAM
19 January 1980: **England 24 – Ireland 9,** Twickenham. *Points scorers – Hare, Scott, Slemen, Smith*

---

2 February 1980: **France 13 – England 17,** Parc des Princes, Paris. *Points scorers – Horton, Carleton, Preston, Hare*

---

16 February 1980: **England 9 – Wales 8**, Twickenham. *Points scorer – Hare*

---

15 March 1980: **Scotland 18 – England 30**, Murrayfield. *Points scorers – Carleton, Hare, Slemen, Smith*

With hindsight, the success probably masked the inherent problems in the English system and only served to delay the subsequent introduction of an English club championship. The following season Twickenham was to witness another Grand Slam, but this time it was the first non-England Grand Slam to be secured on the hallowed turf, as France defeated England 16-12.

The injury to Bill Beaumont that led to his premature retirement in 1982

during a County Championship final at Twickenham was symbolic of the collapse of his England team which had failed to capitalise on the success of the 1980 season. Bill had played 34 times for England since his 1975 debut, 33 of which were consecutive appearances. He had also led the 1980 Lions to South Africa, the first English Lions captain since Bernard Gadney in 1936, and went on to build a media profile as a captain on BBC TV's 'A Question of Sport' quiz programme. He also lost his amateur status after publishing his rugby autobiography "Thanks To Rugby" and agreeing to accept royalties from the book when the rules relating to professionalism wouldn't be bent for him, despite the RFU's annual turnover now pushing close to £2,000,000. He would go on to become the RFU's representative on the IRFB despite being expelled from "the administration, organisation or control of rugby football" in 1982.

Once again the national side fell into a trough of poor results and failed expectation. It does not say much for performances on the pitch when the most memorable events of the period had little to do with the game itself. Erica Roe's

RIGHT England team v Scotland 1980: (Back row L-R) Hare, Dodge, Uttley, Colclough, Scott, Cotton, Neary; (Middle row L-R) Wheeler, Woodward, Slemen, Beaumont, Smith, Carleton, Blakeway; (Front row) Horton

Twickenham streak in 1982 was tabloid heaven. The players, encamped in the centre of the pitch for the halftime interval saw very little of the action themselves, being more concerned with someone in a gorilla suit running full pelt across the pitch towards them. The next month in France, Colin Smart was tricked by team mate Maurice Colclough into consuming a bottle of aftershave at a post match function and ended the evening in hospital.

On-pitch failure led to more concerted attempts to prepare English players for the rigours of higher level competition. The clubs were, other than in the national cup competition, still playing friendly fixtures on a weekly basis. Whilst there was nothing particularly friendly about some of the local clashes, players being asked to make a massive step up in standard when putting on the white shirt of England. In 1984, for example, England went down

ABOVE Bill Beaumont gathers the ball

15-24 against Wales at Twickenham: a record Welsh point score at the ground. How had the five Leicester players in the team (Clive Woodward, Dusty Hare, Peter Wheeler, Les Cusworth and Nick Youngs) prepared for the game? A nine try, 64-9 thrashing of Bedford in a meaningless friendly the previous Saturday. To counter this problem, and mindful of the upcoming Rugby World Cup tournament, the RFU reintroduced the English Divisional Championship, where the elite players were able to compete against each other at a higher level in addition to their club games.

That there could be no quick fix to the ongoing malaise was demonstrated when England conceded a record 100 points in the 1986 Five Nations. In South Africa that summer, a rebel New Zealand touring side (the delightfully named but ultimately despicable 'Cavaliers') were playing their way around the country in direct contraven-

tion of the New Zealand Rugby Union's wishes. Although the exact figures have never been revealed it is believed that the players received a large amount of cash for their participation and the New Zealand Rugby Football Union were quite powerless to stop them. On their return they all took a vow that they had not been paid more than $50 a day expenses to take part in a tour that had generated a kitty estimated to have been $40,000.

England's Marcus Rose was to receive payment in a very different way in Cardiff the following year. The annual battle with Wales was just that, and a particularly vicious one too. As a result of the fighting the RFU suspended Richard Hill, Wade Dooley, Gareth Chilcott and hooker Graham Dawe – a suspension that would give Brian Moore his England debut in the following fixture. So incensed was the home crowd with England's players that they began to hurl their loose change at full back Marcus Rose. A full £3.50 was handed over to the referee for safekeeping before being spent after the game in the bar! Team captain Hill had given an inflammatory team talk that was deemed to have sparked the semi-riot and he was

subsequently stripped of the captaincy. It fell to Mike Harrison to lead the team into the first Rugby World Cup.

The idea of a 'world championship' for rugby union had been floating around for many decades and can be traced back as far as 1906 when, in the aftermath of the first ever Springbok tour of the British Isles, a 'South African gentleman living in London' proposed offering up a trophy to be played for by the great teams of the British Empire. The southern hemisphere nations lobbied particularly hard for the concept because they did not have the benefit of a regular tournament such as the Five Nations and they finally had their way in 1985 with the agreement that a

ABOVE Mike Harrison for England v Japan in the 1987 Rugby World Cup

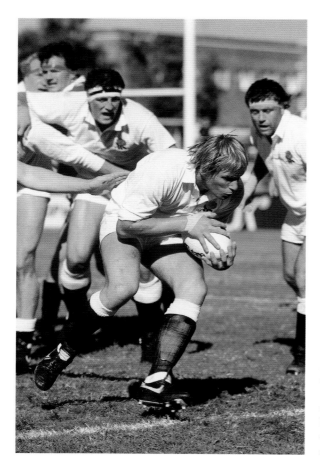

Rugby World Cup competition should be held. The first tournament was scheduled to be jointly hosted by Australia and New Zealand in 1987.

The RFU had been very cool on the general concept, viewing it as another event that would draw sponsorship and, ultimately, the danger of professionalism into the game. No qualifying matches were held for the first tournament and so sixteen teams were invited to attend but it was apparent that the tournament was not taken absolutely seriously by certain elements in the England camp and it was no great surprise when the team was defeated by Wales in the quarterfinals. The trophy was won by New Zealand in front of their supporters in Auckland's Eden Park. It had been a fairly one-sided final against France who had blown themselves out in a thrilling semi-final victory over Australia. The French would do the same thing again during the 1999 Rugby World Cup, but with the two opponents reversed.

An equally significant development occurred in 1987 when the RFU finally bowed down to pressure from many quarters and launched their first league system - the Courage Clubs

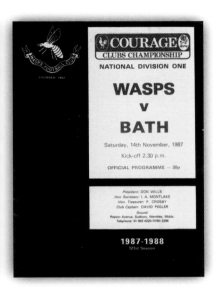

OPPOSITE Peter
Winterbottom carries
the ball against USA in
the 1987 Rugby World
Cup

LEFT The first Wasps
home programme in
the Courage Leagues,
1987

its own 'official' Merit Tables in 1985 but went all the way in 1987 with the league system. The friendly club matches would become a thing of the past and from now on a far more competitive spirit would engender the English game as clubs jostled to win championships, clinch promotion or avoid relegation.

CLUBS IN INAUGURAL COURAGE LEAGUE ONE, 1987

Bath	
Bristol	
Coventry	(relegated)
Gloucester	
Harlequins	
Leicester	(winners)
Moseley	
Nottingham	
Orrell	
Sale	(relegated)
Wasps	
Waterloo	

Championship. The top 20 English and Welsh clubs had introduced their own 'Merit Table' in 1975 in an attempt to add a bit of spice to their friendly matches and to determine the premier club side in a given season. The idea had come from the Coventry club (based on a format already being used by the Sunday Telegraph) and was actually a compromise measure, rather than taking on the RFU in an attempt to start their own league. The RFU introduced

Can it really be a coincidence that following the creation of the leagues and the installation of Geoff Cooke, and his selection stability, at the helm as the first England team manager, England re-emerged, phoenix like, in the late 1980s?

1988-1995

Swing Low, Sweet Chariot

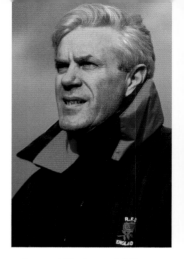

"If England ever get themselves organised, the rest of us could be in trouble"
Finlay Calder, Scotland captain, 1989

WHEN WALES WERE CONVINCINGLY knocked out of the 1987 Rugby World Cup by New Zealand the Welsh manager, Clive Rowlands, was asked what the future held for Wales. His reply was pithy and cheeky: "We go back to beating England". Oh, how that comment must have come back to haunt him in the following decades.

Yorkshireman Geoff Cooke was selected as the first England manager immediately after the first Rugby World Cup tournament in 1987. Although the side had been coached for a couple of decades, team selection was always the

job of the RFU's panel of selectors. Cooke meant to introduce continuity and so he reduced the selection panel from seven to a three-man team that included himself and his coach. With his contract in place and the regular four year cycle of the Rugby World Cup competition established it was possible to work on long term plans for the first time rather than the team stumbling from one season to the next.

The introduction of competitive leagues may have given a fresh impetus and lift to English rugby but the symbolic turning point in England's international fortunes was as unexpected as it was welcomed.

Supporters at Twickenham for the England v Ireland game in March 1988 could have been forgiven for not realising that they were at an epoch-making event, especially at half time. Their team was losing, their captain (Nigel Melville) had been carried off, England had scored one solitary try at Twickenham in the previous two seasons and had lost 15 of their previous 23 matches in the Five Nations. Things were not looking promising. However, out of nowhere, the second half saw an English performance of unbelievable quality. They scored 6 tries – three coming from Chris Oti, making his Twickenham debut – to win 35-3. It was the side's largest points total in the Championship since France had been beaten by a similar score in 1911. In praise of their new hero a small portion of the crowd started to sing the gospel hymn 'Swing Low, Sweet Chariot'. It was a well-known number from the rugby club songbook, complete with dubious hand gestures, and the whole crowd joined in. That could have been that. The day and associated song could so easily have been consigned to memory.

However, the next game at Twickenham saw the first appearance of a new England captain. He was the youngest for a century and was to usher in a new era for the game in England.

LEFT Geoff Cooke

ABOVE Chris Oti, with ball, celebrates one of his three tries against Ireland in 1988

WILL CARLING

ABOVE Will Carling

Cooke shocked everyone by selecting the youngest player in the squad; a player who had missed the first test in Australia that summer to undertake his university exams. Will Carling was the player's name and following a second consecutive great Twickenham victory, this time 28-19 against Australia, 'Swing Low, Sweet Chariot' would be carried forward as England's new battle song. There would be numerous opportunities to air it over forthcoming seasons.

Will Carling was to be the talisman for the fourth great England team and would steer the side to three Grand Slam victories – more than any other captain. He made his debut on the occasion of Cooke's first match in charge, against France in 1988, due to injuries to other players in the centre. His great side would soon include Jeremy Guscott as his partner in the middle and at the outset, as the youngest member of the team, he was very fortunate to have around him plenty of strong, mature

players such as Peter Winterbottom and Dean Richards who were experienced enough to help lead. His side would also star kicking-machine, and future England head man, Rob Andrew; Wade Dooley the six foot eight lock forward; and Rory Underwood who would break Cyril Lowe's England try scoring record in 1990.

Defeats were not met with the massaxing of players that typified the selection process in previous decades and a disappointing draw against Scotland in early 1989 saw Cooke select exactly the same team for the next encounter. A stable nucleus was being allowed time to form.

The first serious attempt at the Grand Slam came in 1990. Eleven Englishmen had been involved in 1989's Lions win in Australia and confidence was high going into the Five Nations campaign. The Ireland team was thrashed 23-0, France lost by what was at the time their highest ever margin at Parc des Princes (7-26) and the Welsh were hammered 34-6. The deciding match was at Murrayfield against a Scotland side also on course for a Grand Slam, although not playing half as impressively. Against a backdrop of political strife and rising

Scottish nationalism the match, dubbed 'the game of the century', took on a level of importance well in excess of that usually awarded to a Five Nations fixture. For the first time the Triple Crown, Calcutta Cup and a Grand Slam all rested on the result of one match. A tough tackling Scotland took all of their kicks and won the battle 13-7.

The game of the century may have been lost, but in subsequent years the England team was to work hard to

BELOW Jeremy Guscott gets to grips with Scotland at Murrayfield, 1990

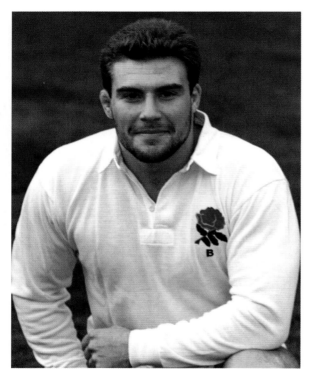

Who could have guessed that in the next five seasons he would play every match in three Grand Slam winning seasons and every game in a World Cup tournament that saw England reach the final? If that was not enough a further decade at the very top level - and far greater achievements - would follow.

The previous season had witnessed stylish rugby but no Grand Slam. In 1991 the forwards would grind out the results. Learning to win with style could wait for a while. The revenge victory over Scotland was sweet, as was a victory from behind with seven minutes to play in Dublin. However the greatest pleasure was finally laying the Cardiff hoodoo to rest. The side decamped to Cardiff a day earlier than usual, all the time listening to loud tape recordings of the Welsh national anthem – determined to be as ready as possible for the atmosphere that would greet them. They were ready, and Simon Hodgkinson kicked seven penalties, to set a record match that Rob Andrew would equal but that Jonny Wilkinson would be the first to better. For a second successive season the final game would be a Grand Slam decider – as the French side was also unbeaten. The match at

expunge the memory. In 1991, especially, there was a ruthless determination that there would be no repeat.

During a summer tour to Argentina a new cap was blooded – Jason Leonard.

Twickenham will always be remembered for 'that' try when the French ran the ball the length of the pitch for Phillippe Saint-Andre to score, yet England were victorious 21-19. The players were carried from the pitch by their ecstatic supporters.

1991 GRAND SLAM
19 January 1991: **Wales 6 – England 25**, Cardiff Arms Park. *Points scorers – Hodgkinson, Teague*

16 February 1991: **England 21 – Scotland 12**, Twickenham. *Points scorers – Hodgkinson, Heslop*

2 March 1991: **Ireland 7 – England 16,** Lansdowne Road. *Points scorers – Hodgkinson, Teague, R. Underwood*

16 March 1991: **England 21 – France 19,** Twickenham. *Points scorers – Hodgkinson, R. Underwood, Andrew*

The rebuilding of England's playing fortunes coincided with the rebuilding of Twickenham Stadium. The first of the new three-tier concrete stands, the North Stand, was erected in place of the old two tier wooden stand. It was

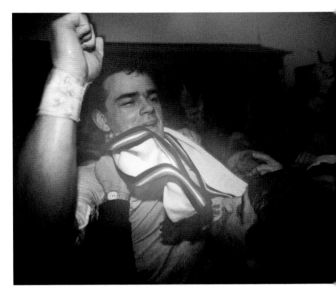

opened in time for the opening match of the 1991 Rugby World Cup tournament. The tournament was held across the Home Nations and France with the honour of hosting the final going to Twickenham. It was a final that England were destined to grace, having demonstrated their superiority in the Northern Hemisphere by defeating France in Paris and Scotland in Edinburgh. In the final they found

ABOVE Will Carling is carried from the Twickenham pitch in 1991 after winning his first Grand Slam

ABOVE England team v Scotland 1991 (Back row L-R) Hodgkinson, R Underwood, Winterbottom, Teague, Ackford, Dooley, Richards, Leonard; (Front row L-R) Heslop, Guscott, Andrew, Carling, Hill, Moore, Probyn

themselves up against an Australia side who were vastly improved in the game since their 'Woeful Wallabies' tag of the early 1970s.

Strangely, England dropped their successful forward-driven game. Many commentators felt it would be too negative a tactic to win and in came a more expansive running style of play. Did they bow to media pressure or were

Cooke and his team simply mindful of the strong and mobile Australian forwards? It might have been that the move was an attempt to out-manoeuvre the Wallabies rather than a nod to public pressure. Either way, the plan backfired, and Australia won the match 12-6, collecting the trophy at the end of the game. David Campese declared afterwards "If England actually played ten-man rugby they probably would've beaten us". England would have to wait twelve years for revenge.

The tournament saw another innovation - the introduction of the first cosmetic changes to the England kit. A blue collar and blue and red hoops on the left arm proved to be unpopular with supporters but the change was another sign of the direction in which the game was moving. Before too long all countries would feature constantly changing distinguishing marks and commercial logos on their playing kit.

Rugby in England reached new heights in popularity as Carling's media profile grew and the success of his team continued. More commercial interest in the game was being generated, which meant the players being denied yet more sponsorship opportunities. They were now professional in all but name – the demands of the modern game requiring previously unknown levels of time and commitment. Long gone were the days of the 1940s when Dr Tom Kemp could do a round of his hospital ward on a Saturday morning before travelling up to Twickenham for an international game in the afternoon.

The IRFB had been fiddling with the

ABOVE Australian players celebrate in the Twickenham baths after winning the 1991 Rugby World Cup

boundaries and definitions of amateurism and the players were starting to agitate for a fair share of the money that was flowing into the game, simply to compensate them for the huge amount of time that they committed.

'Commercial earnings' that still allowed the players to retain their amateur status were under discussion and Brian Moore the fierce hooker who was also a qualified solicitor came to the fore as the major advocate of the England players' position.

ABOVE Wade Dooley and Will Carling model the new England kit in the 1991 Rugby World Cup final

1992 GRAND SLAM

18 January 1992: **Scotland 7 – England 25,** Murrayfield. *Points scorers – Webb, Morris, R Underwood, Guscott*

1 February 1992: **England 38 – Ireland 9,** Twickenham. *Points scorers – Webb, Guscott, Halliday, Morris, R Underwood*

15 February 1992: **France 13 – England 31,** Parc des Princes. *Points scorers – Webb, Morris, R Underwood*

7 March 1992: **England 24 – Wales 0,** Twickenham. *Points scorers – Webb, Carling, Dooley, Skinner*

15 tries and some glorious running rugby are the overriding memory of the 1992 season, as Carling became the first captain in history to achieve back to back Grand Slams. He would play in a remarkable 44 consecutive matches as England captain and after victory against New Zealand in 1993 he also became the first England captain to defeat all of the eight major playing nations. Towards the end of Carling's reign a great captain of the future would debut for the team. Martin Johnson would become the second England captain to complete the full set of major scalps, and would also manage to go one step further than Carling.

Johnson's debut was against France in 1993 as England attempted a unique triple grand slam. The previous autumn a warm up for the assault on the treble had taken place with the first return of the Springboks to Twickenham since 1969. England proved too strong on the day, winning 33-16. The repeal of South Africa's apartheid policies was the reason for their return and also a cause for great celebration. The party would continue in 1995 as South Africa was selected to host the next Rugby World Cup competition.

Before then two other World Cup

competitions would give England rugby a taste of victory. The inaugural World Cup Sevens tournament was held in Murrayfield in 1993 and a young squad including future England captain Lawrence Dallaglio lifted the trophy. At a different location in Edinburgh the following year the England Women would lift their own version of the World Cup, defeating the USA in the

BELOW Celebrations following the second Grand Slam of the 1990s

ABOVE England
Sevens team, 1993

final. The venue was Raeburn Place –
scene of the very first international fixture back in 1871.

Members of Carling's England squad,
although they failed to repeat their
Grand Slam success in 1993, were only
too aware that their on-field success was

generating previously unknown domestic interest in the game. They set up a
company to sign deals with sponsors,
who could then use the players for non-
rugby related activities. Carling said
"more income will go to the players. We
did not receive as much as expected but

everyone is more educated now."

RFU Secretary, Dudley Wood, an unashamed advocate of amateurism, who would leave his post not long afterwards when he saw the direction in which his beloved game was inevitably moving, retained a different view: "Officials and supporters of the game from up and down the country would be appalled at the prospect of players being forced to abandon their careers in order to play the game as professionals"

That summer a record 17 English players, including late replacement Martin Johnson, went to New Zealand with the British Isles. The summer proved interesting off the pitch as well as the IRFB moved to pave the way for former rugby league players to join union clubs.

Halfway through a disappointing 1994 Five Nations campaign Cooke announced that he would be retiring as England Manager, exhausted after over six eventful years at the helm. The reins were handed over to Jack Rowell, who had overseen an extraordinarily successful period at Bath, allowing him a

ABOVE England women, 1994

year to work towards the 1995 Rugby World Cup.

What a selection of players to inherit. Fly half Rob Andrew in particular was on a roll as England's point-kicking machine. Andrew had a great test against South Africa in Pretoria in 1994 where he scored a full house; all four possible types of point: try, drop goal, penalty and conversion. He also kicked all 12 goals against Canada at Twickenham that autumn and would score all of his team's 24 points when

England met Scotland at the tail end of the 1995 Five Nations.

The final match of 1995 meant another Grand Slam decider against Scotland. Unlike 1990 this was to be played at Twickenham and England did not suffer from stage fright. Carling became the first player to ever lead a side to three Grand Slams and it was the first time that England were awarded the Five Nations Trophy – the creation of which in 1993 had necessitated the compiling of a formal Five Nations table for the very first time. There could be no more five-way ties with a prize at stake.

1995 GRAND SLAM

21 January 1995: **Ireland 8 – England 20,** Lansdowne Road. *Points scorers – Andrew, Carling, Clark, T. Underwood*

4 February 1995: **England 31 – France 10,** Twickenham. *Points scorers – Andrew, T. Underwood, Guscott*

18 February 1995: **Wales 9 – England 23,** Cardiff Arms Park. *Points scorers – R. Underwood, Andrew, Ubogu*

18 March 1995: **England 24 – Scotland 12,** Twickenham. *Points scorer – Andrew*

captaincy from him – a matter of days before England were due in South Africa. Carling had the backing of the rest of the team, who publicly declared that none would take up the baton and replace him, and was consequently reinstated three days later following a public apology. England flew out with Carling at the helm to what would turn out to be the last amateur rugby union tournament.

Despite the minor blemish of Ben Clarke being the first ever recipient of a yellow card in an international match (against Ireland) it was a very successful season and the players were feeling confident as the summer's Rugby World Cup in South Africa loomed. Then, two weeks before flying out to South Africa all hell broke loose.

The extra media interest that the game had generated in England ensured that a derogatory off-air comment made by Carling on a Channel Four documentary would create a media storm. When Carling muttered that "you do not need 57 Old Farts running rugby" those 57 (the RFU Committee) moved quickly to remove the England

OPPOSITE Jack Rowell jumps against Martin Johnson in training

LEFT Victory over Scotland in 1995. A third Grand Slam in five years for Carling's men

BELOW Dennis Easby (left) and Will Carling (right) play golf in South Africa during the 1995 Rugby World Cup

1996-2001

A whole new ball game

"To make rugby professional was a gigantic step, because amateurism was the rock on which rugby was built and so many people had insisted for so long that terrible fates would befall the game were that rock to be removed"
Stephen Jones, journalist, 2000

THE 1995 RUGBY WORLD CUP IN South Africa lifted rugby union even higher in terms of media exposure. Nelson Mandela, who had been languishing in prison only five years before, wore a myrtle green South African jersey when presenting the trophy to victorious Springbok captain Francois Piennar. It was an image that spoke of so much more than the result of a determined final match.

After a first ever victory over Australia away from Twickenham,

England progressed to the semi final where a Jonah Lomu-inspired New Zealand ran right through them. That he had a similar effect against Ireland and Scotland in other matches was forgotten as the image of the giant All-Black charging over a hapless Mike Catt to score a try after only 90 seconds was beamed around the world.

Lomu scored four tries as the Kiwis won 45-29. John Mason wrote in The Daily Telegraph of "one player who spent the semi-final of the 1995 World

Cup reducing a previously competent, well-drilled England team, seeking an 11th consecutive victory, to bedraggled also-rans. It was embarrassing; it was also inspiring, a sporting occasion to remember."

The game was now truly a global media event and the threat of breakaway competition finally forced the IRFB's hand. Two Australian media giants, Rupert Murdoch and Kerry Packer had been vying with each other to the sign up the sport and events started to take place at breathtaking speed. Packer's representatives moved from player to player in the Southern Hemisphere, telling them what they were worth in financial terms and then offering them just that. Up to 300 of the world's best players were on board within three weeks. These players had for many years seen money pouring into the game, and into other people's pockets, as a result of their own efforts and exertions and were understandably keen to see some form of remuneration package.

Packer had the players, so Murdoch tried to sign up the unions. However the deal that Murdock's NewsCorp signed with South Africa, New Zealand and

Australia would be worthless if the best players were competing in Packer's breakaway media circus. The key was the South African players and the newly crowned world champions chose to go with Murdoch. Packer withdrew from his enterprise and Murdock had his deal. £370 million was the cost of a 10 year deal that created the annual Super 12s provincial competition and the Tri-Nations tournament.

The amateur game just could not survive under the increased media spotlight and to prevent yet another schism

LEFT Jonah Lomu charges over Mike Catt, 1995

BELOW IRFB minutes declaring rugby union professional

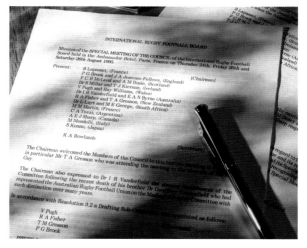

ABOVE Saracens show off (L-R) Michael Lynagh, Francois Pienaar and Phillipe Sella

season that many English clubs had been paying players in cash or in kind for years.

"Although Rugby Union had been ostensibly amateur since its birth, the regulations prohibiting professionalism were not, in practice, enforced. Governing bodies "turned a blind eye" to breaches of the regulations."

(House of Commons Select Committee report into the future of professional rugby, 1999)

It also brought to an end the need for players to hide any contact that they might have had with rugby league. Would the move end the constant, mutually damaging, fighting between the two rugby codes?

The effects of the decision in England were immediate, not least because the change came as a great surprise. The topic had not even been listed on the agenda for that particular IRFB meeting. The RFU had been in negotiation with the England players over a deal which would have earned them £40,000 a year whilst allowing them to retain

the sport had to go 'open' or the IRFB would lose control over large sections of their game. Professionalism was legalised on 26 August 1995 - almost a century to the day since the 20 northern English clubs had broken away from the RFU. The decision saw an end to the shameless 'shamateurism' that had seen certain unions turn a blind eye to match fees, boot money, exaggerated expense accounts, fictitious jobs, win bonuses and (even) salaries. RFU Secretary Tony Hallett had even admitted earlier in the

their amateur status. However, the Union was simply unprepared for full scale professionalism.

It would have been in everyone's best interests for the IRFB to have declared that the game was going to go open in a season or two's time – giving unions the chance to organise themselves. The RFU had debts hanging over them following the early 1990s redevelopment of Twickenham and were in no position to suddenly sign up their top players on central contracts. This is what happened in the southern hemisphere thanks to the funds raised through the NewsCorp deal.

The Union declared a self-induced year-long moratorium before the game in England would go fully professional. Unfortunately it was simply ignored as entrepreneurs stepped in to buy up the major clubs and major players. Saracens had never been a top level club in London, let alone England, yet they soon had international stars such as Michael Lynagh, Philippe Sella and Francois Pienaar in their squad. The RFU's effective management of the situation, at one of the most important points in their history, was nullified by internal power struggles at committee

level and the issue of player-ownership was to be the source of ongoing, damaging, conflicts between RFU and its top clubs over the following years. Alarm bells rang loudly when England players boycotted an international training session in response to a disagreement between the clubs and the Union over funding and the decision-making process in the English game.

England's first match as a professional outfit and the first professional sporting event ever hosted at Twickenham Stadium witnessed future Coach Andy Robinson's last outing for the team and the first 15-a-side outing for Lawrence Dallaglio, as the home team failed to defeat the new World Champions. Each England player in that first season received a retainer of £24,000 and a match fee of £2,000.

Carling announced in his newspaper column that he was stepping down as England captain following 44 wins in 59 games. It had been a tough year for him

ABOVE Clive Woodward is unveiled as new England coach in 1997

which had seen the breakdown of his marriage and increased press interest in his friendship with Diana, Princess of Wales.

The first professional season ended in turmoil and confusion. England contested that having over twice as many member clubs and schools than the other three Home Unions combined should entitle them to a larger slice of television funds, whilst the other Home Unions insisted that the Five Nations was a joint venture and not the property of one country alone. With rumours circulating that the leading clubs might field their own 'England XV' or that England would enter into a global competition with the Tri Nations sides it was announced that England had signed a separate television agreement with satellite television company BSkyB. The deal was worth £87.5 million and the other Five Nations partners were furious - expelling England from the Championship, which led to Twickenham debenture holders threatening legal action against the RFU. Seven weeks later a settlement was reached. As Scotland's Jim Telfer summed it up: "to be honest, Wales, Scotland and Ireland need England more than they need us. They are the country everyone wants to beat."

League was no longer a dirty word at Twickenham, not least because the cash-rich union game with its financial contacts in the City of London could more than hold its own in a market place where for a hundred years league had been able to pick up the best union players unopposed.

Wigan Rugby League Club was invited to enter a side into the 1996 Middlesex Sevens competition at Twickenham and became the very first league side to run out onto the hallowed turf. They won the competition, with future union legend Jason Robinson scoring one of their tries in the final. In 2000 England would play Australia at Twickenham in the first rugby league match to be held at the Stadium.

The first former rugby league contingent joined the 1997 British Isles tour which was also the first major captaincy appointment for Martin Johnson, despite never having held the position for England. It was a wonderfully successful tour of South Africa as the world champions were humbled in their own back yard. However, less than a week after the tour finished 12 of the Lions were included in an England side to play in Australia. Was this the price to be paid for professional rugby - exhausted players and a multiplying fixture list? Unsurprisingly, England lost 25-6 as Jack Rowell coached the team for the last time.

Rowell's part time position was

BELOW Richard Cockerill of England confronts Norm Hewitt of New Zealand during the Haka in 1997

BRING 'EM HOME

AUSTRALIA 76 · ENGLAND 0

Aussies humiliate Woodward novices

TIMETABLE OF DISASTER

upgraded to a full time post and Ian McGeechan and Graham Henry held conversations with the RFU as a replacement for Rowell was sought. It was former Oxford University, Henley, London Irish, England under-21 and (briefly) Bath backs coach Clive Woodward who received the nod. Educated in North Wales, Clive had actually been selected to play for Welsh Schools as a teenager but an injury had prevented him from pulling on the scarlet jersey.

Woodward had a month to prepare for his first four matches. They were against Australia, South Africa and New Zealand (twice) with new captain Lawrence Dallaglio at the helm. It was no great surprise that no victories were forthcoming, but good performances against New Zealand at Old Trafford (where the team went eyeball to eyeball with the All Blacks during their pre-match Haka) and creditable draws with New Zealand and Australia at Twickenham meant that the autumn series produced a genuine feel good factor.

However, the England team were derided in sections of the press following their defeat at Old Trafford for undertaking a 'lap of honour' to thank the supporters for their vocal support. In effect it doubled up as a coded message to the Twickenham faithful. The atmosphere at Headquarters had dipped since the removal of the old wooden stands which had previously towered over the pitch, seeming to sprout right up from the touchline itself. What Twickenham needed was new heroes to shake the crowd out of their stupor, but who would these players be? For the last two minutes of the final game of the 1998 Five Nations

Woodward introduced an eighteen year old back named Jonny Wilkinson.

On the pitch there was selection stability, some great results and a batch of fine young players being blooded. Stability was the last word that anyone would have used to describe the off-field situation. History seemed to be repeating itself on a regular basis. The other Home Unions fought with the RFU, just as they had in the 1880s. The major clubs fought with the RFU just as they had in the 1890s. English clubs did not take part in the first season of the brand new European Cup competition, but instead were involved in the short-lived Anglo-Welsh cup. Major competition sponsors came and went with increasing regularity. It seemed that the only thing NOT attempted was stability. In contrast the major southern hemisphere nations had slipped with apparent ease into their Tri-Nations and Super 12 tournaments.

Thirteen senior players were missing when England toured the southern hemisphere in the summer of 1998 and it was to prove a humbling experience. Seven matches were played and seven matches were lost. The three heaviest ever England defeats were suffered,

ABOVE Blue is the colour. Dejected England players wear 1899 Lions kit against Australia in 1999

including a 76-0 thrashing at the hands of Australia in Brisbane. Christened the 'Tour from Hell' it was a humiliation that Woodward would never forget, although at least he could deflect some of the responsibility since it was Rowell who had set up the crazy match itinerary. It was to mark a distinct turning point in the team's fortunes.

Back at Twickenham the Springboks were prevented from winning a world record 18th successive test victory and

England halted their own sequence of 12 successive games without a win against the Tri Nations sides. It was victory that would set up Woodward's team for their first Grand Slam charge in 1999 – the last year of the Five Nations tournament before Italy came in to create the Six Nations. Victory against Wales on the last day would also give England a record 5th consecutive Triple Crown – having won every match played against the other Home Unions in the professional era. Wales were playing their home matches at Wembley whilst the Millennium Stadium was being constructed in Cardiff and it was Scott Gibbs who scored the injury time try that won Wales a 32-31 victory.

If that Grand Slam failure were not enough for captain Lawrence Dallaglio, much worse was around the corner. An undercover sting by the News of the World newspaper saw him make wild claims about drug use in order to secure a sponsorship deal and he was forced to step down from the captaincy.

Martin Johnson was selected as Dallaglio's replacement and by a strange coincidence his first match in charge was against Australia at the Telstra Stadium where he would lead England to their

LEFT Redesigned England rose featuring subtle 'e' in the middle

finest moment four years later. The match in question was a dubious affair with England dressing up in the red, white and blue hoops of the 1899 British Isles side in a centenary 'rerun' of the very first Australian test match. What the other Home Unions made of England taking on the mantle of the Lions and sewing a rose onto a replica Lions jersey was never recorded. Although the invitation stemmed from an innocent misunderstanding in Australia over the distinction between 'British Isles' and 'England' it was still an inappropriate act

ABOVE A 43-31 victory for France over New Zealand in perhaps the greatest game ever played at Twickenham

the northern hemisphere game.

For the new era a new England rose was designed in 1999 and, fairly symbolically, the RFU were embroiled in an expensive court case over the use of the previous rose. Court cases and infighting were now the norm as battle raged within the top echelons for control of the game. As always, the only real winners were the law firms.

The fourth Rugby World Cup tournament was to be held within the British Isles and France in 1999. This time the final would be held at the newly opened Millennium Stadium in Cardiff – a wonderful venue with a tremendous atmosphere that fell only slightly below Twickenham in terms of capacity. "Judge me on the Rugby World Cup", Woodward told his detractors and that's exactly what history would do - although not in respect to the tournament that he had in mind.

England failed to reach the semifinals, being defeated by South Africa in another new stadium – Paris's Stade de France – in a match remembered for

that simply played to Celtic beliefs of perceived English arrogance.

Celtic frustrations were also boiling over off the pitch where in January 1999 England were again thrown out of the Five Nations following further rows over the distribution of television and sponsorship monies. The expulsion lasted for barely 24 hours, but demonstrated again the underlying tensions in

Jannie De Beer's five incredible drop goals. However, Twickenham witnessed the game of the tournament as un-fancied France defeated tournament favourites New Zealand in a thriller. To witness tens of thousands of English supporters chanting 'Allez Les Blues' in support of arch rivals France was quite something to behold. The Twickenham crowd, as commentator Bill McClaren remembers, "reacted to the magical events placed before them with all the

BELOW Austin Healey is stopped in the Scottish rain, 2000

unfettered enthusiasm they usually reserve for the pride of England."

The calls for Woodward's head after the World Cup were as vociferous as they were predictable, but RFU Chief Executive Francis Baron stood by his man in a gamble that would more than pay off.

Woodward may have failed to get England to the top of the world tree at his first attempt, but surely his outstanding crop of players could dominate the European game in the way that Carling's team had? If he wasn't to be judged on the 1999 Rugby World Cup the public would at least be satisfied with Grand Slams.

But no, England's ongoing attempts to land a Grand Slam saw failure in the last match during three successive seasons. It was as if the other nations were lining up to take turns in derailing Woodward's sweet chariot. Wales had been the nemesis at Wembley in 1999. In 2000 some emphatic victories and equally classy rugby left England to face the potential wooden-spooners, Scotland. However, a side who had even contrived to lose to new boys Italy won a 19-13 war of attrition in the Edinburgh rain. The defeat prompted former captain Carling to

question whether Clive Woodward was the man to coach England: "There has to remain a huge question mark over Woodward's ability to make England a true force in world rugby. My position on Woodward remains sceptical. He has produced a team that can play awesome rugby, especially against the weaker sides, but his England simply aren't winning the crunch games."

The autumn international matches at Twickenham witnessed increasingly assured victories against the southern hemisphere sides and after defeating South Africa in 2000 England would embark upon on a run of just three defeats in the next 41 tests. The 2001 Six Nations again saw terrific rugby and record breaking performances as the side headed towards a final match in Ireland, which an outbreak of foot and mouth disease delayed until October of that year.

Was it a coincidence that talismanic Martin Johnson was absent at the final hurdle for a third successive year as England lost the potential Grand Slam clincher? Ireland fully deserved their 20-14 victory but never has a player looked as miserable receiving a trophy as when Matt Dawson was handed the Six

Nations Trophy after coming top in the table. It was the Grand Slam, and parity with the great England teams of the past, that the side really wanted.

Autumn matches in 2001 included a third successive victory over South Africa and a record 134-0 demolition of Romania that featured 20 England tries. England's qualities were increasingly evident. Woodward was building the fifth great England side - the greatest of them all.

2003 and all that

"When they ran on to the field it was like watching a tribe of white orcs on steroids"
Michael Laws, New Zealand journalist, 2003

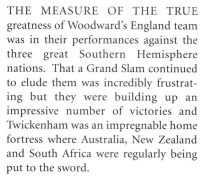

THE MEASURE OF THE TRUE greatness of Woodward's England team was in their performances against the three great Southern Hemisphere nations. That a Grand Slam continued to elude them was incredibly frustrating but they were building up an impressive number of victories and Twickenham was an impregnable home fortress where Australia, New Zealand and South Africa were regularly being put to the sword.

As preparations began for the 2002 Six Nations the law of averages decreed that it was probably France's turn to deny England a Grand Slam, and so it proved. It may have been the third game in the series rather than the last, and it

may have come a week after England found themselves at the top of the IRB's world rankings, but the frustration was not diminished. A subsequent 50-10 victory over Wales – a result that would have woken the dead in previous decades – was a relatively subdued affair once the Grand Slam had gone begging again. It demonstrated quite dramatically how far England had come.

Woodward was trying his utmost to gain that extra 1% for the England team and no stone was left unturned, no idea was considered too crazy.

The England dressing room was now a far cry from the plain, uninspiring, grey breezeblock affair of the seasons prior to Woodward's tenure. He used

carefully considered imagery, colour and key phrases ('The pride and Tradition of England will not be entrusted to the timid or weak', 'Every great success was achieved with enthusiasm. Nothing was ever achieved without it' and 'You may have to fight a battle more than once to win it') to turn it into a place of perfect psychological preparation.

Tricks were also played on visiting teams. Allegedly the mighty All Blacks were held up outside their Twickenham dressing room whilst someone disappeared to 'try and find a key for them'. Was it a delaying tactic to put the great side off their stride and make them feel less special or is it simply a myth? The

fact that it is entirely believable speaks volumes for the environment the head man was creating at Twickenham.

Although the following year would see them reach the pinnacle of their success, Martin Johnson's England probably reached their playing peak in the autumn of 2002 when they took on and defeated New Zealand, Australia and South Africa on successive Saturdays at Twickenham. The first two were tight affairs but an out-of-sorts Springboks

LEFT Jonny Wilkinson

BELOW Players in the England dressing room, 2001

were destroyed 53-3 – their heaviest ever defeat. It was the first time that a northern hemisphere team had beaten all three of the southern hemisphere giants in a single season and it laid down a marker for the following year's Rugby World Cup in Australia.

This time the Grand Slam just had to be delivered, and once again England reached the final day of the season needing just one more win. Before them stood an undefeated Irish side looking to emulate their heroes of 1948 and win a second ever Slam. Martin Johnson's belligerent attitude just before the playing of the national anthems when he flatly refused to move his team at the behest of a flustered Irish official perfectly summed up the team's state of mind. They were not in the mood to bow to anyone – even if it meant that the Irish Prime Minister had to leave her red carpet and walk on the grass. It was a moment which said so much about Johnson and his team. A strong Ireland side were crushed 42-6 and Jason Leonard had finally gained his elusive fourth Grand Slam to join the club that contained Cyril Lowe, Dave Davies and Ronald Cove-Smith. Heady days indeed.

2003 GRAND SLAM

15 February 2003: **England 25 – France 17,** Twickenham. *Points scorers – Wilkinson, Robinson*

22 February 2003: **Wales 9 – England 26,** Millennium Stadium. *Points scorers – Wilkinson, Greenwood, Worsley*

9 March 2003: **England 40 – Italy 5,** Twickenham. *Points scorers – Lewsey, Wilkinson, Tindall, Luger, Thompson, Simpson-Daniel, Dawson*

22 March 2003: **England 40 – Scotland 9,** Twickenham. *Points scorers – Wilkinson, Robinson, Cohen, Lewsey, Grayson*

30 March 2003: **Ireland 6 – England 42,** Lansdowne Road. *Points scorers - Wilkinson, Greenwood, Tindall, Dallaglio, Luger, Grayson*

The young Jonny Wilkinson, a metronomic kicker of unbelievable dedication scored points in every game. By the end of the season he held twelve different England scoring records, including the most points scored in a Championship season (89) and most points scored in a Championship match (35). He had

already scored more points than any Englishman in the history of the game, but his finest moment was still to come.

The strangest thing happened next. England undertook a short tour of New Zealand and Australia and, rather than watching fearfully through their fingers or hoping that the score would still be respectable at half time, the England support were actually looking forward to the Test matches and the opportunity to secure a second ever win on New Zealand soil and a first on Australian soil.

Both were achieved in wonderful style and the most memorable period of play was undoubtedly in Wellington

OPPOSITE Jannes Labuschagne of South Africa is sent from the Twickenham pitch in 2002

ABOVE This time it's a Grand Slam: Lansdowne Road, Dublin in 2003

Australia's Telstra Dome in Melbourne was the first game ever played by England under a closed roof.

By now the statistics were astonishing. Ten straight English victories in matches played against the big southern hemisphere giants and 30 victories in the last 33 international fixtures.

That England narrowly lost a Rugby World Cup warm up match in Marseille, 17-16, was disappointing. A record 14 match winning streak was ended but the game is best remembered for the first outing of a totally new England kit. Nike had designed a, Woodward inspired, light weight, figure-hugging top which was a massive departure from the previous heavy cotton jersey. The jerseys themselves were literally falling off the England players' backs by the end of the game as they battled with a French team also wearing the same new design. Tongue in cheek conspiracy theorists pointed out that both sets of kit had been manufactured to (allegedly) identical specification... in France. Less amusing for Jason Leonard was that it now took at least two people to help him take off his tight fitting top after each match!

In a return leg of the friendly against

where a six man England scrum on their own five metre line (following the yellow carding of Lawrence Dallaglio and Neil Back) managed to repeatedly hold back the might of the full strength All Black pack. A 25-14 victory in

France, Ben Cohen scored a try in the 45-14 Twickenham win making him the first England player in history to have scored a try against each one of the other Six Nations teams and all three of the Tri-Nations sides. Lawrence Dallaglio and Richard Hill would both match the feat the following season.

The team flew out to Australia for the 2003 Rugby World Cup on 1 October as favourites but their progress through the tournament was not always convincing. An inexperienced Georgia side was crushed, the Springboks were brushed aside, Samoa posed a tough challenge and the Uruguay team was thrashed in the pool stage before the Welsh were faced in the quarter final.

BELOW The forwards clash in Wellington during 2003's famous England victory

The side was not always playing brilliantly, but were at least doing enough to win. A scare against Wales saw the men in scarlet finally overcome after the introduction of Mike Catt and his expert tactical kicking. A rain-soaked semi final victory over France at the Telstra Stadium witnessed Jason Leonard's world record breaking 112th England cap and there were strange goings-on in the other semi final between the hosts and New Zealand.

Both sets of fans would boo and whistle to drown out occasional outbreaks of 'Swing Low, Sweet Chariot' that signified just how many English were in the crowd - happy to have obtained a ticket for any game and by now desperately trying to secure one for the final.

A crowd of 82,957 packed into Sydney's showpiece stadium for the final match and no-one could have predicted the drama that was to come. Andy Robinson was later to confess that England's success that day was due to two factors. The first reason was that, thanks to their medical team, England had an entire squad of 30 fully fit players to select from. The other aspect was that after the selection process of the starting 15 was made the very first players on the training field at the next session were those who had missed the cut – supporting and congratulating the others.

The memory of the match itself, for the majority of English supporters, will probably be a tense blur. It was the most tightly fought of contests; the two teams matching each other kick for kick and try for try. Extra time was entered into and the commentators had started to dip into their competition rule books to see how the post-extra time penalty shoot-out would work. As the clock ticked down towards zero, the most dramatic finale occurred. Martin Johnson

BELOW Ben Cohen pounces on the ball to score against France: the first Englishman to score a try against all of the major rugby nations

ABOVE Jason Leonard takes the field to win his 112th cap

ENGLAND TEAM IN THE 2003 RUGBY WORLD CUP FINAL

15 – JOSH LEWSEY
14 – JASON ROBINSON
13 – WILL GREENWOOD
12 – MIKE TINDALL
11 – BEN COHEN
10 – JONNY WILKINSON
9 – MATT DAWSON
1 – TREVOR WOODMAN
2 – STEVE THOMPSON
3 – PHIL VICKERY
4 – MARTIN JOHNSON (captain)
5 – BEN KAY
6 – RICHARD HILL
7 – NEIL BACK
8 – LAWRENCE DALLAGLIO

Replacements
MIKE CATT (for TINDALL)
JASON LEONARD (for VICKERY)
IAN BALSHAW (for LEWSEY)
LEWIS MOODY (for HILL)

and Matt Dawson moved the ball into a favourable position for Jonny Wilkinson to drop for goal, with mere seconds remaining, on his least-favoured, right foot...

Frenzied scenes greeted the team after their early morning arrival at Heathrow airport and an open top bus tour around central London attracted close to one million people out onto the streets. Drinks were had with Tony Blair at Number 10 Downing Street and tea was taken with the Queen. The winner of the BBC TV Sports personality team of the year award was never in any doubt and the acres of press coverage occasionally stepped over into the ridiculous: 'Is Rugby the new Football?' asked at least one headline.

Steve Thompson had played in a record 15 England matches during 2003 and Lawrence Dallaglio was the only England player to have been on the

BELOW Jason Robinson scores in the Rugby World Cup final

pitch for every second of the entire tournament, but such details were irrelevant. It was Jonny Wilkinson fever that swept the nation and he was afforded the sort of idol worship usually reserved for pop stars and soccer players.

Every aspect of his character and training regime was examined and particularly revealing was the revelation that he focussed his kicking in training by aiming at an imaginary woman sitting behind the posts. The imaginary woman acquired the name Doris at some point and, having hit Doris, he would then try to hit an imaginary ice-cream in her hand and then eventually the flake in the ice-cream!

The Sun newspaper set out on a quest to recover four of the balls used in the World Cup final and bring them back to England. Following an extremely expensive operation one was given to a Sun reader, one to the Museum of Rugby at Twickenham, one to Jonny Wilkinson and one to Martin Johnson.

A great advantage for the RFU was that the competition was won at the beginning of the domestic English season and so every opportunity could be taken to utilise the media exposure. The trophy was toured around the country, seen by an estimated 2,000,000 people over the following two seasons as interest in the game boomed.

A MORI opinion poll suggested that 16 million adults were now interested in rugby union compared to 10 million adults prior to the World Cup – a massive increase. Within a year over 33,000 new players had been recorded in England and new clubs were being formed. A year later the number had grown to 50,000 new players (a remarkable 25% increase), ending a player drain that had been exacerbated by the

LEFT Ben Cohen looks on as Wilkinson scores THAT drop goal...

BELOW England team with trophy, 22nd November 2003

ABOVE A media scrum as England bring the trophy back through Heathrow Airport

RIGHT A small number of the hundreds of thousands who filled central London for the victory parade

Martin Johnson had officially retired early in the New Year. It was the perfect way to end on a high, but his departure still left English supporters mourning. The only man in history to have captained the British Isles on two tours had also led England onto the field on 39 occasions, 34 of which ended in victory – a statistic which is, unfortunately, never likely to be bettered. Others were on their way out, including the player who had started more games under Woodward than any other – Neil Back. Back was unceremoniously dumped from the squad, a decision which Woodward would later publicly regret. Endless shoulder and groin injuries were to turn the Wilkinson fairytale into the Wilkinson injury saga and commentators were soon wondering if a kicking machine who had only ever experienced one defeat in 27 Twickenham internationals would ever play for England again.

A drab victory over Scotland in the

advent of professionalism and the lure of watching rather than playing rugby.

The present was bright and the future looked rosy. Could Clive Woodward (sorry, Sir Clive Woodward) lead England to become, in 2007, the first side to ever successfully defend a World Cup title? Only one previous winning team (Australia) had progressed as far as the final in the next tournament. Woodward led the team into the 2004 Six Nations and everything just started to collapse.

2004 Six Nations suggested that all was not well and this fear was confirmed when Ireland won at Twickenham – England's first defeat at headquarters in 22 matches stretching back to 1999. What was the cause of this post World Cup hiccup? Was it too many experienced players departing or too many of the old guard left hanging around? Was it exhaustion or apathy? More importantly, how soon could it be shaken off? Defeat in France gave them the Six Nations crown and England's period of dominance was on the slide.

Another sad departure occurred in 2004 when Jason Leonard trundled off the pitch for the last time. 'The Fun Bus' had won a world record 114 England caps and his balance sheet showed 86 victories. Quite incredibly he had faced the new champions, France, on 18 separate occasions.

The following season would determine if the national team was suffering from a hangover or from something worse. The omens were not good when Clive Woodward acrimoniously resigned from his position – citing lack of access to the best club players as an aspect that made his job, and a successful defence of the World crown, untenable.

The reins were handed over to his coach Andy Robinson and the 2005 Six Nations Championship saw things slip even further for the World Champions as defeat in Wales was followed swiftly by defeats at home against France and in Dublin against Ireland. A poor season where England came fourth in the Six Nations was summed up by the sight of 18 year old Mathew Tait, awarded his debut in the caldron atmosphere of the Millennium Stadium against a pumped-up Wales, being picked up off his feet and driven yards backwards by Gavin Henson.

Robinson's second Six Nations tournament was little better than the first and 2006 saw Scotland join the growing list of teams to have beaten the reigning World Champions, alongside third successive victories for both Ireland and France. The completion of the South Stand at Twickenham and the final part of the evolution of the home of England rugby into a 83,000 seat bowl was cause for celebration, but there was not too much optimism looking forward to the defence of the World Cup title in France 2007, even when Rob Andrew came on board as the RFU's first ever Elite Director of Rugby.

Incredible highs and lows had been experienced in such a short period of time, but it was no different to many other eras in England's history. The great 1892 side decamping en masse to the Northern Union; the first England side to be whitewashed in the Five Nations championship winning on New Zealand and South Africa soil; Carling's

Grand Slam champions being walked over by Jonah Lomu. Swings and roundabouts; ups and downs.

So what about the great curse of professionalism? What terrible fate has it bought upon the game in England? Harlequins, the archetypal English rugby union club, the club of amateur stalwarts Adrian Stoop, Ronald Poulton-Palmer and William Wakefield, now field a rugby league side playing in the Super League. If this is the very worst that professionalism has to offer then the game's future is pretty secure.

BELOW 2006 Guinness Premiership launch

The pictures in this book were provided courtesy of the following:

GETTY IMAGES
101 Bayham Street, London NW1 0AG

MUSEUM OF RUGBY, TWICKENHAM
Rugby Road, Twickenham TW1 1DS

Book design and artwork by Newleaf Design

Published by Green Umbrella

Series Editors Jules Gammond & Vanessa Gardner

Written by Jed Smith